The Pack Goat

The Pack Goat

John Mionczynski

Illustrations by Hannah Hinchman

PRUETT PUBLISHING COMPANY
BOULDER, COLORADO

Printed in the United States
10 9 8 7 6 5 4 3 2 1

Library of Congress Cataloging-in-Publication Data

Mionczynski, John, 1947–
    The pack goat / John Mionczynski : illustrations by Hannah Hinchman.
        p.   cm.
    Includes bibliographical references and index.
    ISBN 0-87108-828-2
    1. Pack goats. I. Title.
SF387.M56   1992
636.3'912—dc20   92-16298
                                                      CIP

Cover and book design by Jody Chapel, Cover to Cover Design, Denver, Colorado

Whether your wether's a fair weather wether
Or whether he weathers the storm,
Hither and thither or whither you wander,
Together you'll never go wrong.

Photograph courtesy of Jerri Oster

Contents

Acknowledgments viii

Introduction 1

1. Why Pack a Goat? Or How to Get the Monkey
   Off Your Back 4

2. Breeds 26

3. Goat Hairs in My Couscous (Life on the Trail) 38

4. The Pack String 66

5. Food Along the Trail 74

6. Hooves and Dewclaws 81

7. Capricorn 85

8. When the Heat's On: Desert Goats 89

9. Glacier Goats 96

10. Training 102

11. Acquiring and Keeping Goats: Home Sweet Home 117

12. On the Technical Side: Historical Notes 127

Selected Reading 139

Index 140

Acknowledgments

When I began writing this book, I did not think of myself as a writer. I still don't. I did feel the need, however, to share with the rest of the world some of what I've learned about goats as amiable beasts of burden. To the extent that this book is readable, I owe a debt of gratitude to Kathy Buchner for her psychic abilities in transcribing into understandable English my original, penciled-in, hieroglyphic manuscript, compiled during one long stay in the desert; to Debby Donahue for sanding off the rough edges (very rough, in some cases); and to the artistic genius of Hannah Hinchman, who made the goats in this book jump from the pages and take form.

Mostly, I'm grateful to the long list of those who taught me what I know about working goats: Brownie; Sweetpea; T.C.; Alpi (wonder goat of the Rockies); Jupiter; Menu; Julio; Twolio; Newlio; Shorty; Bob; Penny; Heidi; Jessie and her kid James; Curly; Toglockenshire; Chauncey; Fido (actually spelled Phydeaux) and his brother Rover; Nameless; Jessica; Tiny Tim; Yate; Casper (the friendly goat); Django; William (the conqueror); Cocoa; Bud; Blossom; Jade; Flash; Amigo; Stretch; Entré; Gimpy; Spot; Sparkle; Farfle; Unic; Gypsy; Raz-Ma-Taz; Rudolph (the red-nosed goat); Morgan; Greenpeace; Zeus; Big Guy; Mindy; Jessica II; Butthead; Penelope;

Alfonse; Blacky; Moran; Targhee; Silver; Lophead; Beekins; Jake and Elwood; Rosebud; Andy; Goatius Maximus; and many many more. And of course Wethervane, my first pack goat.

Introduction

GOAT (gōt) *Capra hircus* 1. any of numerous agile, hollow-horned ruminants of the genus *Capra*, of the family *Bovidae*, closely related to the sheep, found native in rocky and mountainous regions of the Old World, and widely distributed in domestic varieties. (From *The Random House Dictionary*. New York: Random House, 1967.)

This is all you need to know to begin reading this book. In fact, you'll do a lot better if you dislodge from your gray matter any other preconceived notions (including facts) about goats you've acquired. I don't care if you've operated a goat dairy for the last forty years, most of that knowledge won't amount to a hill of nanny berries as far as the pack goat is concerned.

In the following pages I'll be discussing an animal that is experienced in the backcountry, in tune with its instincts, strong, hardworking, intelligent, loyal, disciplined in the skills pack animals have been trained in for thousands of years, and one more thing—*friendly!* (In all the years I packed horses, I didn't know one you could call friendly—good-natured, maybe—tolerant, sure—but not *friendly*, at least not in the same way a goat is friendly.)

Of course, not all beasts in the genus *Capra* can be described by the glowing adjectives above. Many of us have childhood (or later) memories of

1

goats or, more likely, conjectural impressions that tend to generate adjectives such as nasty, stinky, cantankerous, devilish, sneaky, and some that can't be printed.

I once knew a devoted woman who, at the time, was milking seventy to eighty goats a day once in the morning and once in the evening. She loved her animals but referred to them affectionately as "barn potatoes." And that they were! As in most dairies I've visited, these goats were lazy, overweight, poorly muscled, crotchety, uninspired, uninclined toward anything resembling work, and untrained with two very dairy-oriented exceptions: one, you could set your watch by the goats lining up at the feed trough for breakfast; and two, all seventy-some goats would stand in line and come through the door to the milking room in the same order every day. The sixty-seventh doe to come through the door yesterday would be number sixty-seven today (goats learn these sorts of things very quickly). Other than that, these poor caprids lazed in the sun all day unless it rained, in which case they'd get up and move 20 feet into their spacious barn. It's a good thing they hadn't discovered TV.

We've all seen similar behavior traits in human kids. Some are industrious, bright, and eager to work; others watch TV all day and scream at the slightest suggestion of helping their parents. What's the difference? Obviously, it's the early training they receive. Or, to put it another way, what they're allowed to get away with. Later on we'll see why pack goats aren't nasty, stinky, cantankerous, devilish, or sneaky—or, on the other hand, maybe why yours is. It depends mostly on what happens to them before they are six months old. From here on, it's important to remember that goats are very much like people. Kids will be kids, whether they have horns or not.

Down through history, the poor goat has been blamed for man's mistakes. It's true that goats have a unique ability to eat and digest woody plants, as well as about any other kind of vegetation. This, combined with their tenacious desire to keep on living (called "survival instinct") and high reproductive rate, has caused large tracts of land to be denuded of shrub cover and changed into desert. But we seem to forget the reason goats were there in the first place: Humans put them there to convert overgrazed scrub land into edible protein (goat meat and milk) because cows couldn't survive there, having eaten all the available grass. The trees were gone as well, having disappeared long before in clouds of smoke from cooking fires. The goat was merely the last step in the long drawn-out process of overusing a region's natural resources (this process is called "desertification"). The process repeated itself all over the Middle East, Africa, and the Mediterranean. And in every area a university expert would put his magnifying glass to the barren ground and exclaim, "Ah ha! Goat droppings!"

Sometimes goats weren't even involved but were only innocent bystanders. For instance, when large stands of trees (eucalyptus, olive) were planted to replace exhausted supplies of firewood or as quick cash crops to boost a stumbling economy, the resulting disappearance of native ground cover caused devastating erosion and loss of land. Goats were blamed. Sometimes the cause was overgrazing by sheep, but guess who took the rap. Even in the Bible, the sheep sit at the right hand of God and the goats sit at the left hand. (Of course, I've raised goats for a long time, and I've never seen one sit at all—they stand or lie down. So I take this to be some kind of metaphor.) Anyway, it should be clear from all this why you never hear of a scapecow or a scapechicken. It's always a scapegoat.

Well, times are changin'! As more people are exposed to working goats, word is spreading that the goat may just be the most wonderful, loyal companion a man or woman can have, especially in the wilderness. (And besides, if things really start going haywire back at camp, you always have someone to blame it on!)

■1■
Why Pack a Goat?
Or How to Get the Monkey
Off Your Back

I KNOW what you're thinking: Why not a horse or llama or mule or donkey? Because goats are practical, efficient, inexpensive, easy to handle, unintimidating, easy on the environment, and good company. They can negotiate terrain that no other pack animal can. In addition, does (female goats) can not only pack, but supplement your grub box with a very tasty milk from which you can make yogurt, hot chocolate, and even cheese in the backcountry (and all more digestible than cow's-milk alternatives).

Let's analyze this question a bit and see if you're a legitimate candidate for goat-packing.

There is an ever-growing number of Baby Boomers who get up in the morning and struggle out of bed holding our lower lumbar regions, awakening to the realization that having spent all of our free time for the last twenty years trudging up and down mountains with a heavy backpack may not have been the smartest thing to do. The sad part is that we'd do it all over again, given the chance. Well, here's the chance. Most of us can still hike. It's the monkey on our backs that gets to us. What if we let the monkey ride a goat?

After about age thirty, we all begin getting shorter. Our bones aren't getting shorter—it's the discs between our vertebrae that lose some of their elasticity and compress. This isn't caused by a chemical in the air that no

4

one can pronounce. It's perfectly natural and caused by the effects of gravity. Carrying a heavy pack on your shoulders puts more pressure on these discs, making them compress even more. Falling, slipping, and tripping all add impact to the extra pressure, and that's worse yet. In addition, carrying a pack exerts unnatural downward pressure because it sticks out behind you instead of up above. So those little discs don't settle straight down, neatly sandwiched between the vertebrae. The backward pull of the load and compensating forward pull of your shoulders makes those discs ooze out one side and squash down on the other. You don't notice these things when you're young and indestructible. But sooner or later the mask is lifted and pain creeps in. Just offstage the wheelchair is waiting.

Come to western Wyoming and watch an old horse-packer walk down the street and you'll see that packing horses isn't any better. Packing horses is fun, glamorous, and exciting—or so some think. But try packing ten to twelve hours a day, seven days a week, as I did, and the fun, glamour, and excitement wear off in about a week. After a month it's more like a desk job without the desk. Sitting all day staring at a mess of horseflies attacking your pony's withers is not really all that good a form of exercise, either. You do work some muscles riding a horse, but it's not exactly what you'd call cardiovascular exercise. The cardiovascular exercise you do get comes when you least expect it. Packing horses is akin to Mark Twain's definition of adventure: long hours of boredom interspersed by moments of stark terror. I have at least one slipped disc and a broken vertebra to attest to that.

I also remember a time when my pack horse went down in a mud hole way back in the mountains. The mud was halfway to his back and he was heavily loaded. My saddle horse couldn't pull him out, so I had to dig into the mud and get under his belly to unhook the lash rope and cinches and completely unpack the 150-pound load. It took half a day and a mud bath before my saddle horse could yank him out.

At times like that you realize what a large prehistoric remnant the horse is. If he weren't so darn functional for the human race, he'd have gone the route of the giant ground sloth and other Miocene monster mammals. There is no question that the horse has survived because he was the all-around best pack animal, and later, private and public transportation system to come along. And he still is, for many kinds of work. But there are times and places when the horse may not be the most appropriate animal for the job. Much as I loved working with horses, there came a time when practicality demanded a change.

This is the age of appropriate technology. Not because we're into appropriate technology today and ancient people weren't. People have always been interested in appropriate technology. But today there are so many more options to choose from in almost every aspect of living. So many, in fact, that finding what works best for us as individuals may take a little head scratchin', a bit of study, and an investment of time.

I live two miles from the boundary of a national forest nicknamed "the horse forest." I've seen scores of people get into horses here. There is always more than one reason for this, but chief among them more times than not is the perceived glamour or image of the horse—perhaps coming from the person's past, probably the influence of childhood TV programs. The horse seems an eminently practical pack animal to these folks, and in some rare instances it is. But in most cases horses are rejected after a few years and always for very practical reasons: they're too expensive to feed, they require too much land to keep, they generate too many vet bills, they're too much work, they take too much time.

What these people are really saying is that for them the output didn't justify the input; owning a horse was not appropriate. That's why there are horse-packing outfitters. They pack your stuff in on their horses, you can ride the horses if you like, and the outfitters worry about the rest. For most people it's cheaper to do it that way. It takes about one to two years for a new horse-packer to realize that there's more to it than walking down the trail with a beast of burden who gleefully carries your gear for free.

First of all, it's not free. The animal may cost anywhere from $500 to $1,500 to acquire. A person can easily spend $1,000 on a horse in one year, even if he already has a good place to keep him. Hay can cost $100 a ton, and a horse can eat 5 tons a year. Then there are the annual vaccinations, worm medicines, food supplements, and farrier bills (horses have to be shod to work in the mountains). Next come the unanticipated injuries and illnesses that add to the unpredictable annual veterinary expenses. Finally, you get in the mountains and make the shocking discovery that, to use the analogy of the car, you are not only the driver but the mechanic, tow truck, gas-station and parking-lot attendant.

Yes, horses eat grass, but these days grass is scarce and most public-land jurisdictions require that you pack in at least some supplemental horse feed. In some places you must pack in *all* the feed for your animals. A horse eats about 25 pounds of grass a day (that's 100 percent of his net load capacity for six days), and you have to camp where there's enough grass to eat. Furthermore, if you pack long enough, your horse will eventually throw a shoe. If you don't replace it, you risk damaging the hoof or even laming the horse. This is more serious than a flat tire, because the effects can be permanently disabling. To rectify the problem you need to know how to trim the hoof and fit a new shoe. You also have to carry the new shoe with you on the trail, along with the nails and tools to fit it—about 6 to 10 pounds of metal, depending on how good a job you want to do.

A humane packer should also carry a handgun in rough country to quickly dispatch an animal with a broken leg or other serious injury when getting him out of the hills is out of the question. I've heard several gruesome tales of putting an animal out of its misery with a big rock. (The stories were gruesome because this technique rarely works the first time.) The other option is to unpack the poor critter and simply leave it. (You wouldn't want to stay around and witness its starvation.)

It's usually a panicked horse that breaks a leg, drives a stick into its flesh, or gets tangled in an old roll of barbed wire hidden in the bushes in somebody's hunting camp. Many horses tend to panic easily when something seems unfamiliar. A responsible horse-packer always carries an emergency vet kit for just such eventualities, and a knowledge of how to treat wounds. I got lots of use out of my vet kit, not only in treating my own horses but more often in treating animals belonging to other "horse-packers" who probably had a good supply of aspirin and bandages, but who neglected to bring any horse medicine.

For some, a horse or donkey is the perfect pack animal, but for most who try either, it's a short-lived fantasy.

If you're contemplating alternatives to backpacking, you need to sit down and figure out how many days a year you plan to use the backcountry and how big a load in terms of weight and bulk you need. Then you need to decide what kind and how many animals you will need to get you (and your family or friends) and your gear into the backcountry. These days I often see families or hiking parties using one pack animal to lighten everyone's individual load.

Then you need to decide if you really need to *own* a pack animal or animals. Figure it out: If a pack animal costs you $800 to buy and $1,000 per year to keep, it may not be worth your while to have one around all year to use for your annual two-week vacation. It would be less expensive to rent one. (If you do rent, make sure it's an animal you can handle and one that won't restrict your itinerary.)

Llamas are good pack animals whose limiting factor for most of us is their purchase price. Llamas usually cost more than a good pack horse, sometimes considerably more, but they are cheaper to feed—about one-quarter the cost of feeding a horse. Goats are by far the least expensive pack animal to buy and maintain. In my area, you can buy about six pack goats for the price of one llama, or three goats to one horse. And llamas and goats are more versatile than horses, donkeys, or mules in that they both can negotiate more difficult terrain and eat a wide variety of wild vegetation, so that you can camp virtually anywhere and have acceptable pasture for the night. Goats are a little more versatile than llamas in this regard because they eat all the things llamas eat plus a wide variety of

woody stems and dead bark not on the llama's preference list. This is what the goat is most noted for in world history—surviving in places where virtually everything else had been starved out by overgrazing.

As a pack animal, the goat is most noted for surefootedness. It's true that a llama can keep on going where a horse is locked in by rugged or rocky terrain. But the goat isn't even into his element until long after the llama has said *Whoa*. Total ease in rugged, out-of-the-way places is the goat's number-one advantage. Besides being able to negotiate it, goats are most at home in that type of terrain. When caprids were first domesticated, they were taken from the wild crags and cliffs of the rugged mountains of the Middle East and Central Asia. The instincts born there are still with them. This is where a good pack goat will really impress you. A pack goat can go where no other pack animal can go.

It's this fact that led me to the discovery of goat-packing in the first place. At that time (1972), I didn't know that a goat could be packed. All I knew was that I had a job I was very excited about, and I wanted to figure out a way to get it done. I was employed by the U.S. Forest Service and my job required that I follow and stay close to a band of Rocky Mountain bighorn sheep to observe and record their food habits and behavior in the wild. I had a good deal of equipment to pack into the mountains: spotting scope, tripod, binoculars, technical books, two-way radio, tent, clothing, food, and a bulky, strange-looking device for tracking the sheep called a radio receiver. These sheep had been fitted with radio collars, and my link to them if they decided to migrate was my receiver. No one had ever done radio-telemetry studies on bighorn sheep before, so most of what I was doing was experimental. Even the receiver—a big aluminum box with a copper loop on top—was experimental. The slightest jar could cause it to malfunction, and back to town I'd go (that would take several days). This was a common event in the early days.

Well, I started out using horses, but that didn't work very well. The horses did a good job of getting my base camp in, but they couldn't get near the terrain where the sheep lived. So when the wild ones moved on to new places, the horses were worthless. Worse than that, they were a pain in the neck. There wasn't enough grass in that country to leave them picketed anywhere for more than a day, and if there was such a place, I'd have to come back every day to move or water them. Totally inappropriate.

So the horses went, and I started backpacking. Carrying any backpack in that terrain was dangerous enough, but one time in town I weighed mine. It was over 100 pounds! So I got rid of some food and ate more wild plants. But the pack was still too heavy.

I was at a level of desperation when, after a particularly difficult day in the mountains, my mind conjured up the image of a goat loaded up like a pack horse. I don't know how you react to that idea, but I couldn't help laughing out loud for a while. It was absolutely ridiculous, but remember—I was desperate. So when I got home for a few days off, I tried it. I had several goats at home (I've always been fond of goat milk), and I had a harness goat I used to haul water on a travois from a creek to my cabin. I knew old Wethervane could pull a couple hundred pounds on a travois using an old upside-down horse halter for a harness. But I had no idea how he'd react to a load on his back. I started slow, using the saddle bags from my riding saddle, slowly adding more weight as I walked him around. It was as if nothing were on his back. So I got some bigger bags, loaded them with some of my gear, and slung them over his back with a horse pad for padding. It worked. This was getting exciting! After a day of walking this eleven-year-old wether (a wether is a neutered male goat) around with ever-increasing loads on his back, I could see that with just a few refinements I could probably take him back to the mountains with me. One refinement that proved necessary was a rough saddle-tree made from some one-by-six boards and a sawed-up shovel handle for crossbucks. It quickly became clear that with a saddle to distribute and stabilize the weight the old goat could carry a good deal more. We were already up to 45 pounds.

Back in the mountains, old Wethervane followed faithfully and silently. He was so quiet that I could let him stay with me at camp and even at my

observation post. He didn't alarm any wild animals. He was a Toggenburg (one of the brownish colored Swiss breeds) and looked like just another wild beast of the mountains. (This was ultimately his downfall: Wethervane was shot the opening day of deer season several years later.) But Wethervane's true test came the day the sheep decided to migrate. Could he keep up? It started before daybreak. The radio signals were clear—we were on the move! Wild sheep can go thirty miles in one move, and I had no idea where these guys would end up. Well, we hiked several days along escarpments and over mountains, and although my buddy had a few new things to learn, he performed beautifully. I was ecstatic. You *can* teach an old goat new tricks!

Each day Wethervane worked he became stronger and could carry more weight. I could see his muscles growing and firming up. (He was starting to resemble a horse, but his horns would always give him away!) He was looking trim and fit and athletic. Goats have to develop the muscles that horses have naturally because of their different ways of dealing with predators in the wild. Horses have to be ready at a moment's notice to outrun predators, maybe for miles. Their muscles have to be stout enough to carry an 800-pound animal several miles at forty miles an hour. Goats are equipped with muscles that allow them to run a short distance and then bound up to a cliff ledge where predators can't get at them. Their musculature doesn't have to be as massive, but it can be developed, just as in people. Just picture a desk jockey (an accountant, for instance) standing next to an Olympic athlete. As babies, both had the same physical potential; it was the time spent in development that makes the difference in their bodies today.

In time, I was packing Wethervane, Jessie (my milk goat), and several kids as trainees. Soon I was watching my goats with the same trained eye that was observing the wild sheep: The similarities were encouraging. There were forage species everywhere used by males and barren ewes for body maintenance. Then there were special plants selected for milk production. Some were selected by young lambs for fast growth, and some, I found out later, for inhibiting parasites. The selection process was the same for goats and sheep. For example, Jessie could maintain a relatively high milk production on a wild diet high in bitterbrush, and she knew how to select for it.

Fresh goat milk in camp and on the trail was an exciting fringe benefit, and it was that much less food I had to pack for myself. Besides, it was delicious. Goat milk is a milk-drinker's delight: sweet, rich, and more agreeable than cow's milk. I learned to make yogurt in the mountains before I made it at home. Just heat the milk a little above body temperature (around 110° Fahrenheit), pour some into a quart jar with a couple tablespoons of an active yogurt culture, and place it in a sleeping bag for five hours. While you're looking through the spotting scope (or fishing) you're also making yogurt. When it's done, I like to add a few wild thin-leafed huckleberries. Life doesn't get a whole lot better than that!

But my greatest pleasure came from seeing how healthy, alert, and handsome (how much like a wild animal) a goat can look when it's being worked. Also how much like a wild animal it can act: testing the air for scents, twitching the ears, looking around, curious about every new sound and scent and movement. A different animal entirely from the slothlike potbellied barn potato.

That's how it all began. More and more people are becoming aware of goats, so let's take a quick look at the common categories of people who become goat-packers.

Researchers. First, in my mind, is the scientific researcher. I have used goats on the job for this kind of work for years, both in the government's employ and for my private studies. I'm very impressed with this amiable creature who follows you around close at hand with all your tools and references, as well as all your camp equipment, so that you can be

free to poke around and do your job, whether it's mapping plant communities or collecting specimens. Both professional and amateur scientists and naturalists have used goats to collect habitat information, scats, and acid-rain samples from rugged mountains where the other option would be a $700-per-hour helicopter. They have been used to pack in scientific study camps beyond the reach of pack horses and llamas, and they have packed specialized equipment such as rubber rafts for high-elevation lake studies and delicate equipment such as glassware, microscopes, plankton nets, electronic instruments, solar panels, batteries, and two-way radios. With care, all these things can be transported via goat without damage.

Families. Families with young children find goats a safe and fun way to get in all those extras you need (but don't get any help carrying) with young kids. Some families have told me that if it weren't for the "rent-a-goat," they just wouldn't go in the mountains until their children grew up. Children as young as two years have been able to accompany parents on week-long wilderness trips with goats. I once watched a two-and-a-half-year-old boy lead a five-goat pack string (carrying a total of 230 pounds) for several hours. He loved it!

Some of these parents told me they'd tried llamas first but had some personality conflicts between the kids and the animals. The llama is certainly big enough to be intimidating to some youngsters. Also, llamas just aren't as friendly as goats, and goats are easier to handle in camp. I know some couples with very young children and even babies who own one or two goats so that they can carry the little ones on their own backs and put all their equipment on the goats.

Furthermore, goats can be trained to neck-rein just like a horse and, on a pack saddle with a little padding, a youngster in the proper weight range can ride a goat. This, of course, requires a reliable, well-trained goat and a mature, responsible child, but I've seen children ride all day long down the trail. Verbal communication can also be used to direct a saddle goat. Needless to say, a good deal of caution should be used by the parents. Make sure the trail is not strewn with boulders the child could get hurt on should he or she fall. Always use a very calm, well-trained animal who's not prone to spooking. Keep the saddle cinched down tight. Some kids really take to this right away, and it can be a chore to peel them off the goats when it's time to make camp.

Here again, the addition of fresh, good-tasting goat milk and yogurt is a welcome treat for children and adults alike.

Climbers. Another person attracted to the advantages of the pack goat is the avid hiker, including the mountain climber. Those who go to the mountains frequently and who like the idea of a pack animal find the goat a good way to lighten their loads and still get off the trail into more remote country. Secondarily, the goat makes a pleasant hiking companion who enjoys being with people. You can talk to your goat—he may or may not listen—but there is a bond, and it can become very close. In addition, your companion can get you across those remote boulder and scree fields that lead to the high peaks and climbing faces.

I said that the companionship of the goat is secondary to what he can do for you. It's interesting to see how these priorities change with some people after they have traveled with their "beast of burden" awhile. Repeat-renters often ask for a particular animal by name. One of my customers once inquired about renting a goat for the next week. I told her I could rent her a goat but that Jupiter, the one she usually rented, was already working that week. She decided not to go until some future date when Jupi could make it.

Education. For several years the National Outdoor Leadership School (NOLS), based in Lander, Wyoming, has contracted me to lead pack strings on some of their wilderness skills courses to assist in carrying a portion of the class's load. Instructors find this works well for certain types of field courses. Generally, six of my goats carry all the food, fuel, and some climbing gear (about 300 pounds) for about fifteen people. We can go right up the side of a mountain with this arrangement, making it a little easier on the students who, after all, are there to learn, not to break their backs.

On one of these trips I had an exceptional goat named Julio. Julio is one of those goats who loves to cuddle up against your sleeping bag at night. He'd loiter around while everyone was bedding down for the night. If no one called him over, he'd pick someone, slowly appear out of the darkness, and politely stand by his or her sleeping bag. If he wasn't chased off, he took it as an invitation. Carefully, silently, and with great accuracy he would kneel down and then lean over until he was comfortably snuggled against the warm sleeping bag. Goats cuddle with other goats on cold nights, and some like to share warmth and closeness with people. If you have never slept with a goat on a cold night, you don't know what you've been missing! One night, making camp with some NOLS students at the base of Wind River Peak (about 11,000 feet), we all knew it would be a cold night. I had to chuckle because I could hear a group of women arguing over who was going to get Julio that night. He was definitely a hit!

Goats are successfully being used for other kinds of educational trips, including ecological and botanical studies and desert archaeology, and have proven to be very handy for carrying some of the more cumbersome teaching aids you wouldn't normally take into the field, as well as the food and camp gear for overnight classes. For years I have used goats to assist in my own field courses on biological and survival subjects in both the desert and the mountains. Freedom from heavy backpacks and the chore of managing animals makes a four- or five-day field trip much more pleasant. And the presence of good microscopes and necessary (heavy) reference books makes for a better learning experience.

Senior Hikers. As people age, they often quit doing certain things, either because they have to or because they think they have to. Backpacks are no longer feasible, and horses are too much trouble. It's a joy to see people who had quit striking out for the backcountry return to it with a goat. An animal that willingly follows behind with all your gear, feeds itself, and is easy to handle when the need arises, extends the time a person can go on long hiking trips.

I'll never forget a particular trip up to the Continental Divide in the Absaroka Mountains of Wyoming. We were looking for the elusive nest of the black rosy finch, which no one had ever photographed. Our guide was Mary Back, the well-known and much-loved naturalist of western Wyoming and the widow of Joe Back (who wrote, among other books, a highly acclaimed guide to horse-packing: *Horses, Hitches, and Rocky Trails*). Mary was then eighty-one years old. Other than accepting an occasional hand from "us youngsters," Mary hiked along just fine at her own pace, certainly an inspiration to the rest of us.

Mary had done more backpacking than a lot of hard-core backpackers, and more than her share of horse-packing, having operated a dude ranch in Dubois, Wyoming, for many years with her husband in the 1930s and 1940s. At this point in her life, Mary no longer felt secure around horses, and she was not as surefooted as she once was. Using my goats as pack animals freed her from the unstabilizing burden of a backpack and allowed her to focus her efforts on being a naturalist. We all learned a great deal from this wonderful woman. She became quite fond of "her" goat on this trip, Jupiter, and of all the goats really. She thought goats were the most reasonable answer to the dilemma of growing older and still wanting to pack in the wilderness. As she put it, "I wish I'd found out about goats when I was a lot younger."

The American Elder Hostel recently started conducting some educational/recreational field programs that use goats to carry lunches, water, and extra-warm clothes on day trips for the seniors. Two goats for a group of twelve are plenty. The response to the goats has been outstanding. The participants seem to appreciate a gentle animal that is content to just tag along with the group. Those who collect specimens can have them carried out by goat power. Furthermore, a goat can be trained to come when its name is called, a handy trait when a resting Elder-Hosteler needs a sip from the water bottle.

All in all, the older person and the young, eager goat are a perfect combo, whether for an overnighter or a quick jaunt to the corner store for groceries. Some seniors are now buying pack goats to help carry things on hikes as well as for company at home. Due to the time spent on imprinting and gentle contact when they're young, pack goats are a source of amiable comradeship and love for their human companions. (This isn't necessarily true of goats not trained for packing.)

The Disabled. Working goats are ideal for people with a wide variety of disabilities. A relatively small, easy-to-handle animal, a goat can be managed by someone restricted by injury and for whom a backpack is out of the question. I've seen victims of certain types of paralysis make good use of pack goats where larger animals were too risky and a backpack unreasonable. For many types of physical injury, walking—but definitely not with a pack on one's back—is the best therapy. One of the most satisfying stories of goat-packing I've heard concerns people in wheelchairs who were using goats to pack into the woods via "wheelchair trails" (specially built for wheelchair access). Apparently, goats are just the appropriate height for someone to handle from a seated position. What a wonderful use for these wonderful animals.

Because goats respond so well to early training, I can see the day when goat carts will be driven on, say, bicycle routes by the disabled and elderly, whether for pleasure or into town for groceries. The load capacity ratio of pulling to packing for a goat is about five to one. Thus, a goat that can pack 60 pounds can pull 300 pounds by cart or sled. They are easily trained to adapt to cars, people, and noises, and will respond well to verbal or hand commands. For more information on using goats to pull, you may want to subscribe to the publication of the British Harness Goat Society: Mrs. Anne Cox, Cornwall's Hill, Lambley, Notts NG4 4P2, Great Britain.

Hunters. If you're the type of hunter who goes after mountain goat or wild mountain or desert bighorn sheep, or if you simply like to hunt in those rocky crags away from the war zones, you may find the goat is the only option to your own back for getting your meat out. It takes several trips or several goats to move an entire elk, but it can be done. Two goats can carry out a bighorn sheep in one trip. (Other advantages of having goats along on hunting trips are discussed under "Outfitting.")

Photographers. I don't hunt anymore, but I like to stalk the wily portrait. Most large animals living in the wild are intensely curious about the appearance and smell of the pack goat. Many will approach within 10 to 20 yards, ignoring the human presence, just to get a closer look at the four-legged newcomers. In fact, some will follow your pack string for miles. In addition, the goat's eyesight is seven times our vision in distance. Packing with a goat is like walking around wearing binoculars. A seasoned pack goat who's been in the wild country a year or two can spot animals a mile away or the flicker of an ear from a bedded animal long before you

can. He is sensitive to the slightest hint of something that may be a threat or kin. Pay attention, and you'll learn to read his mind. Look for a long, motionless stare with eyes open wide and slightly bulging, ears far forward and focused on the target, followed by a staccato gurgle coming from the throat. This is a warning sound and will normally get any other goats staring in the same direction. If the hackles go up along the topline (the area along the back from the croup to the shoulders) and the back of the neck, then the sighting is interpreted as a probable threat (coyote, dog, bear, or large animal that is too close, such as elk or a herd of wild horses).

Tip: Many wild animals won't interpret you as a threat if they can't see you from the waist down. Keep your legs behind your goat and photograph at will while the animal approaches. Sometimes you can zigzag toward a wild animal while keeping your legs hidden behind goat panniers. Some of my most exciting wildlife experiences have happened just this way. It's fun even without a camera.

And by now you know a goat can carry all those lenses, camera bodies, film boxes, and tripods you hate to lug along on your back.

Outfitting. From personal experience, I can tell you that outfitting with goats is a viable, practical, unique, and low-overhead way to run a commercial packing operation. I've found it seems to generate its own business by word of mouth with a good, healthy percent of return customers, whether for fishing, recreation, education, or contract hauling. Many people want to get away from the overcrowded, easily accessed areas of the backcountry. Others want to try something new and unique. Goat-packing appeals to both these groups.

Commercial contracts, whether private or government, have a ready clientele in some areas simply because there may not be any other affordable alternative. Goat transport is cheap, especially when compared to the costs of a helicopter. An outfitting concession in a rugged hunting area where deer or wild sheep are not easily hauled out on horseback, for instance, may be a fairly busy seasonal venture.

To get into commercial outfitting, you need to check with two authorities first: one, the state or local outfitters association for its rules and regulations; and two, the landowner or managing agency where you plan to work—local district offices of the U.S. Forest Service, Bureau of Land Management, National Park Service, state agency, or private landowners. Each will have its own local or regional restrictions, policies, and regulations. Make sure you can comply with all the applicable requirements, especially insurance minimums. Or you may want to work for an established outfitter. He can handle your insurance and a lot of the jurisdictional paperwork, and maybe even some advertising. You can pay him a percentage of your gross income—ten percent is a reasonable figure. You will essentially be a guide employed by him and this will save you getting the outfitter's license, which can take time and money.

Converts. Some of the most devoted converts to goat-packing are former llama-packers. The same general reasoning that enables a person to see a llama as a viable option for packing also applies to the goat. Both are small, easy to handle, and easy to transport. A single animal can carry all the gear one person needs for a one-week- or two-week-long trip. Both have a wide range of food habits, allowing you to camp almost anywhere, and both can negotiate terrain inaccessible to horses, mules, or donkeys.

Better than half the llama-packers who, out of curiosity, have taken goat excursions with me have gone on to sell their llamas and acquire pack goats. Others preferred their llamas. To each his own. But among those who converted, the pattern was very similar. Driving to the trailhead, they would tell me how great llamas are and how unlikely it would be that they'd be swayed enough by my goats' performance, no matter how impressive, to trade in their llamas. Most would add that there's no place a goat can go that a llama can't! (Mule- and donkey-packers are famous for that last statement, too.) By the end of the first day they would often comment on how surprisingly capable the goats were. By the end of the second day they would start bringing up their llamas' shortcomings. And by the end of the third day we would be discussing the price of goats.

Following are some of the primary differences between llamas and goats that I've gleaned from seasoned llama-packers:

1. Llamas generally pack slightly more weight than do goats. Although I keep hearing that some llamas will pack up to 140 pounds, I have yet to see one do this. Most llamas are packing net loads of 50 to 85 pounds in the mountains. This is close to what I'm packing on my goats. On average, I'd guess that llamas carry about 10 to 15 pounds more than do goats. (Many llama-packers tell me they'd never put more than 50 pounds on their animals for a long trip; others say a llama in good condition will pack 80 to 100 pounds of mountain cargo.) For a long trip in the mountains, the upper limits for goats vary from 50 to 80 pounds.

2. Llamas can handle rough terrain quite well. But goats can, without question, handle much rougher terrain as well as unstable terrain (teetering rocks, slippery and sliding surfaces).

3. The average initial cost of a llama is about a thousand dollars more than that of a pack goat. If you're interested in breeding llamas to produce your own, you can increase that figure to $3,000 to $6,000 per breeding animal. At this point, you have to decide whether you want a Jeep or a Cadillac.

4. It is universally agreed that pack goats are more pleasant animals to have around camp and are easier to handle, doubly so because they

don't tend to run off when left untied for long periods. In fact, if they're raised and treated properly, goats generally don't have to be tied up, even at night.

5. Goat food habits, although similar, are more varied than those of llamas. Goats tend to eat very little grass in the mountains, easing the pressure on overgrazed mountain meadows.

6. It is a disputed question how many miles a loaded llama will do in a day in the mountains. Most estimates range from fifteen to thirty miles. Goats normally top out at around twelve to fifteen miles if they're in good condition. My all-time high was eighteen miles up and down mountains in 2 feet of snow with a string of nine goats. We were all tired at the end of that day! (In the Wind River Mountains of Wyoming, where I "road-test" my goats, backpackers rarely do more than eight to ten miles in a day, and six miles is often a long day. So these kinds of statistics can be misleading.)

7. Pastured at one campsite, gelding llamas tend to produce large scat piles by returning to the same spot over and over. They also tend to defe-cate in the water while crossing streams. Goats don't have these tendencies.

To some pack-goat owners (myself included), a doe pack goat that can produce 240 gallons of milk plus a new batch of baby pack goats every year is a valuable investment that in a year can pay back the entire initial investment in goat, pack equipment, and feed. Bear in mind that a 240-gallon-per-year goat is a low-production doe, which is what you want for a pack goat. A high producer will put out upwards of 500 gallons of milk a year (about 1-1/2 gallons per day), and will snag every stick and stub in the path with her udder. Such an animal should never be used for packing because it would be painful and dangerous to her health—and very impractical. A goat with a large, pendulous udder cannot walk properly for long distances, and her high protein requirements would seriously limit her working endurance. Five hundred gallons of milk is enough—let's not ask any more of the old girl!

There are more people than you'd think who would take long walks with their goats, just because they are such good company, before they realized you could pack one. I hear this all the time. Some of these people even experimented with packing their animals with saddle bags or similar arrangements. What a surprise to find out you can put a saddle on your goat and take along all sorts of things just in case—like a raincoat, water jug, sandwich, camera, flashlight, binoculars, field guides, accordion— and still walk free. Even small goats and milkers can be used for day walks like this. I like to take a walk in the evening over the hills behind my place with a group of goats (thirty or forty). There's a certain feeling of peace and calm you can pick up walking with goats after a hectic day—a meditative,

pastoral feeling that sets you right with the world again—just you, the goats, and the planet Earth.

Goats that are bonded with humans are very affectionate—affectionate to the degree that their human counterpart is affectionate. If you spend a lot of quality time with your goat a strong bond develops, almost like that with a pet dog, yet different. The goat stays out at night and feeds as an independent animal. But he or she knows when it's time for knoodling (pronounced ka nōōd ling). He will stand by you, staring off in the distance, but sensitive to your slightest movements. If you sit, he's likely to come over and stare in your face: This means "pet me." Goats love to be petted on the neck, especially the sides, have their jowls scratched, have their head scratched behind the horns (or behind the knobs on disbudded, or hornless, goats), and be fondled, brushed, hugged, and talked to.

Each goat is different in his preferences and will express them by presenting various parts of his anatomy subtly (and sometimes not so subtly) before you. Most pack goats are very gentle yet expressive. If an individual wants his neck rubbed, he may lower his head and horns, so as not to touch you with them, and walk forward, raising his neck to touch your hand. Some goats face you, look you in the eye, and slowly raise a front foot to get your attention. Some even gently lay that hoof on your leg or arm. A working goat knows not to do those things during working hours

Photograph by Frandee Johnson

(whatever they might be) but will expect some knoodling when the work's all done. He will understand if you're too busy and have to put it off a day or two. Just a few words will appease him. He will become very sensitive to your ways and patterns, more so than other herbivorous animals. This is partly due to the goat's intelligence and partly to his loving nature. Train him right, treat him right, and you'll have a good friend. You cannot beat a goat into submission as you can a mule and expect him to perform!

Let's talk dough—not nanny doe—but dough, moolah, $. A common response to the idea of acquiring a pack animal is, "I don't have the money to buy an animal." Well, let's look at that. Prices change, but in 1992 you can buy a fully trained, packable yearling wether for $200 to $350. Most people, however, opt to get a greenbroke pack kid (about six months old, sold by a recognized pack-goat breeder) for $100 to $175 and work with him themselves. In that case, you're paying principally for the special breeding plus some early training. Taking your kid on hikes, getting him used to wearing panniers, leading him on a lead rope, and training him to come when his name is called are all easy and fun to do, so why pay someone else to do it with your goat? After the age of six months, most "training" consists simply of getting packing experience. You can purchase all you need to pack your goat (saddle, saddle pad, panniers, collar, and lead rope) for under $250. So if you're halfway frugal about it, you can be set up for $350 to $400. Have you priced a new backpack lately? Then there's all the specialized, high-priced, lightweight gear that goes with it. And don't forget to factor in the chiropractor bill. For that same $400 you can just about buy all the rig you need to pack a horse. But then you still need to buy "Ol' Paint," and he's not going to be cheap!

All things considered, a pack goat is the least expensive way to hike unburdened. Furthermore, although prices vary, renting a pack goat is still cheaper than any other rental option. At this early stage in the evolution of commercial goat-packing, it may be difficult to locate a Rent-a-Goat outfit. As time goes by this will become easier, but for now you can look in the yellow pages of the phone book under "Dairy Goats" or just "Goats" and ask the goat breeders listed for some direction in your particular area. Be prepared for laughter or long periods of silence on the other end of the line. But don't give up—sooner or later someone will tell you where to find what you're looking for!

A question that often arises is, "Can my dog hike with a goat?" That's not usually a problem—it all depends on the dog. Working goats get used to almost anything, and sometimes a goat and dog will really strike up a friendship. The owner of the goat you're renting will have to decide what is appropriate when he or she meets you and Rover. (As with other pack-animal-rental outfits, you may have to appear in person for a friendly interview to make sure you don't belong to some ancient Hebraic cult practicing animal sacrifice—goats have a history of being heavily selected for that sort of function—and to sign some standard type of waiver for liability purposes.)

One final note for you skeptics who can't get rid of the mental image of the goat as a wimp. Let's look at the statistics: Depending on the terrain, temperature, build, mileage, speed, and experience of the individual animal, a pack goat carries twenty to forty percent (gross) of its body weight. The average for a well-conditioned pack goat is thirty percent. The relatively small size of the goat actually works to its advantage for this reason: Speaking in terms of species, as the size (mass) of an animal increases, its load capacity in terms of body weight decreases slightly.

There's one more thing to consider: feed. All pack animals eat a little more when they're working, and as you might expect, this amount increases dramatically with larger animals. But since I don't have solid figures for a working diet, let's just look at maintenance figures, that is, the amount of feed consumed by an animal to maintain its body functions. These figures vary a lot depending on the type of feed and its condition, but it's safe to say that a large wether eats approximately one-fifth what a horse eats just to maintain itself (and this percentage is probably lower

Photograph by Frandee Johnson

when both the horse and goat have been working hard). The average pack goat is carrying one-third the net cargo of an average horse (goat—50 pounds; horse—150 pounds). So the goat is doing more work for the same amount of feed—forty percent more work per pound of feed! Or, stated another way, the goat is forty percent more efficient at getting a given amount of cargo from point A to point B (if the distance is within the maximum range of the goat for one day). If you're interested in going more than twelve to fifteen miles in a day, well, you may want a horse. However, as the world's supply of grasses dwindles, particularly in the backcountry of our public lands, the horse may still not be the most appropriate choice. And don't forget, a beast is not a Buick! When you park him at the end of a trip, he continues to burn fuel—all year! Since three goats carry what one horse carries, you can keep one "horsepower" of goats for forty percent less money, no matter how many days you actually use them.

This forty percent efficiency figure has two implications: One, the goat is easier on the environment because, simply stated, he's eating less of it while getting the same job done; and, two, you're paying less for feed to move any given poundage of cargo. And if you're truly concerned about the environment, the forty percent efficiency factor is only the beginning. What the goat eats as a ruminant browser includes leafy broad-leaved forbs such as dandelion and thistles. There is a strong preference for tough woody plants like willow, understory shrubs, and tree twigs, as well as leaves, needles, and bark—both dead and alive. Although there may definitely be some localized environmental concerns with this diet, the overwhelmingly noticeable effect is to take the pressure off the uncommon and precious grass meadows and displace it to the abundantly common woody species of most backcountry areas. These foods are naturally selected for by goats and contain a good deal of cellulose (though less than grass). Because the goat is a ruminant and can take up to four days to process his food, he can digest and utilize sixty percent of the cellulose in these plants, as compared to forty percent digestion by the horse. Add to this the goat's special ability (unique even for a ruminant) to physically break down tough plant parts in its digestive system, plus its ability to produce protein by recycling urea, and the result is that, under working conditions in high-cellulose environments, the goat is actually performing closer to fifty percent more efficiently than the horse while using a much more appropriate habitat. Now that's environmentally sound!

Try this experiment to prove the goat's superiority as a food-digester to yourself: Feed some whole oats in the normal ration to a cow (another ruminant) and a goat. Wait the appropriate time and examine the droppings. There will be no sign of oats in the goat raisins, but almost every single oat grain will be evident in the cow pie.

▪2▪
Breeds

IN THIS CHAPTER, I will very briefly describe the major differences between the recognized American breeds of goats to assist the prospective goat-packer in selecting the right animal for a particular job. In this book's final chapter, you'll find more technical information on this subject, but for now a general overview is all you need.

There are eight major breeds of goat recognized in the United States and Canada: Toggenburg, Saanen, Nubian, Alpine, Oberhasli, LaMancha, Angora, and Pygmy. In addition, there are a few minor breeds such as Cashmere, Kinder, and Pygora. All can be packed. For obvious reasons though, we can eliminate some of these from consideration as practical pack animals. Size is a limiting factor in two specific areas: load capacity and length of leg.

The Pygmy and Kinder breeds are bred chiefly to be small and cuddly. They make wonderful companions for people with small backyards, and the Kinder can even produce a milk supply on less feed than other breeds require. But since you can put only a third of their body weight (an average for all goats) on their backs, these little guys could carry only 8 to 20 pounds. Then subtract the weight of an 8- to 10-pound saddle, saddle pad, and panniers, and you're somewhere between overloaded and a 12-pound net-load carrying capacity. Not efficient!

A team of Angoras being used as draft animals during one of the last gold rushes in Alaska. *Photograph by E. A. Hegg; reprinted by permission of Special Collections Division, University of Washington Libraries, neg. no. 2TH.*

The same generally holds true for the Angora (a short-legged hair goat originally from the Middle East that produces mohair), which generally tops out at 80 pounds (net load capacity of 16 pounds), and the smaller Pygora (a cross between the Pygmy and the Angora). This does not mean they can't work. Larger Angoras have been used very successfully as draft animals.

Now the Cashmere (a Middle Eastern/Asian hair goat that produces—you guessed it—cashmere) has much better possibilities, reaching weights of 150 pounds. But it was bred to be short-legged. A short-legged goat has to take more steps than a longer-legged goat and thus can't go as far in a day—it flat works too hard. (This rule applies to any pack animal.) It would be interesting, from a packer's perspective, to see the American Cashmere growers breed for longer legs. It's always nice to get two uses out of anything functional—a philosophy common to people who spend a lot of time in the backcountry. (I have a button accordion I usually take everywhere and inside of which I've built storage containers for an emergency medical kit and extra food. That way it never feels like excess baggage.) Cashmere goats have their hair collected twice a year. This process takes about an hour each time, but they eat 365 days a year. Seems like they could be doing something with their spare time.

Saanen.

Aside from a possible application in recreational spelunking, we can disregard the Cashmere, Kinder, and Pygora and get on to breeds of more promise for the serious goat-packer. The following comments refer primarily to wethers, which are most commonly used for packing.

Saanen

Pronounced saw-nen. From the Saanen valley in Switzerland, these goats are usually large (bucks are sometimes over 300 pounds). Long- and short-legged bloodlines are common, and individuals of both are often big-boned and sturdy. Horns are large at the base, long, tan in color, scimitar-shaped, and deeply ringed. This breed's disposition for packing is perfect —super-mellow and quiet, virtually silent on the trail and in camp. These animals are impressive, often packing up to 85 pounds in easy terrain and 60 pounds in steep, rocky terrain. The lovable personality is a strong plus. Saanens are most serviceable in alpine elevations and at cooler temperatures.

Saanens can have two problems: One, except for the rare sable color, Saanens are pure white with pink or mottled skin. A pink hide and pure white hair is linked to a tendency to overheat in hot weather,* and this

---

*In caprids, it is not uncommon for behavioral and physiological distinctions to be linked to specific pigmentation patterns, for instance, excitability and tongue color in bighorn sheep (*Ovis canadensis*).

Toggenburg.

holds true for Saanens that have been crossbred with other breeds. Two, some bloodlines tend to be prone to weak pasterns. Generally, this should not be cause for concern if the goats come from a genuine pack-goat breeder, because a breeder would naturally cull those bloodlines. A weak pastern is a trait that may not appear until the goat is two or three years old, and it might not show up at all. From my experience, fallen pasterns of the hind feet, although hereditary, often seem to require lack of exercise as a prerequisite. Therefore, most working goats just don't show signs of this problem if they work a fair amount of the time. This also holds true for range goats that are allowed to play freely and that inhabit good, rocky goat habitat. Dairy goats show the trait at a fairly predictable genetic rate of occurrence because most dairy goats are confined and in dire need of exercise. (There are several other physical and physiological problems occurring commonly in farm goats that just don't affect working goats, and we'll learn more about some of these things in Chapter 11.)

Toggenburg

This is another Swiss breed (the oldest recognized breed of goat) similar to the Saanen, with identical horns. Toggenburgs are brown with white (sometimes yellowish) facial stripes, lower-leg markings, and rump patch, with a dark hide. Generally, Toggs have strong legs and strong pasterns, but beware of short-legged strains (they're more common in the western states). Wethers should be at least 34 inches high at the shoulder when four years of age.

Toggs are less mellow and more independent than Saanens, especially as they get older. Along with these traits comes an advantageous wariness in the woods. This breed makes for an excellent watch goat who is not noisy but will stare in an alarm posture. I've been able to make countless wildlife sightings by keeping an eye on my Toggs and Togg/Saanen crosses —sightings I'd have missed without that Togg watchfulness. Furthermore, a goat's night vision is remarkably acute. A small tinklebell on a Togg around camp at night will keep you aware of intruders (animal and human) beyond your own senses. Once you get used to watching your hiking buddy in the wild, you'll be able to guess in general terms what he's seeing by his reactions.

Never lose your temper with or abuse a working Togg, either in the training phase or when the goat is an adult. These are very sensitive critters who enjoy their independence. They are loyal, but from a distance. I have a Togg that always runs off just out of reach when I appear with a saddle in my hand. I have to talk to him and cajole him and walk around after him for a while with an outstretched hand. When he's ready, he'll let me grab his collar and saddle him. Thereafter, he is a model pack goat until we get to our next camp and take off his saddle. Then he goes off to a high rock close to camp and stares at me. This is typical behavior, and merely a Togg's way of stating his independence. All my Toggs have shown this behavior to some degree. Be accepting. They're worth your patience!

One more tip. If you have a mixed pack string, gather up all the Toggs first (and any skittish goats) and tie them up before bringing out the saddles. This makes the goat-packer's life a little easier. Once in the pack string, your Toggs will have greater endurance and heat-tolerance than your Saanens.

Alpine

Alpines are often called French Alpines. Most of the specimens you'll see in this country are American Alpines; that is, French Alpines crossed into other bloodlines and bred to maintain some of the traditional French Alpine traits. In general, Alpines are fine-boned and a little smaller than Saanens or Toggenburgs, but since the late 1970s the trend among many dairy breeders has been to quest for the monster Alpine—and that is good news for the packer.

Alpines resemble the Swiss chamois, with a long, more angular snout (like many wild goats and goat-antelopes), and distinctive, shorter black

Alpine.

horns that are sometimes more tubular than the flattened scimitar shapes found in Saanens and Toggenburgs. In fact, I believe there's a strong possibility of some genetic mingling of chamois with Alpines in recent times. A wide variety of color patterns occur. Some of these are recognized as standards by the American Dairy Goat Association and have strange names, such as Cou Claire, Cou Blanc, Sungau, and Chamoisee (a color pattern with many similarities to the wild chamois). Some individuals are even pure jet black. The color is of little significance to the packer, but is of importance to the pack-goat breeder because the prettiest ones usually sell first. Alpines are very attractive animals with white and/or black facial stripes and a wide variety of patterns mixing black, white, gray, and brown. They are very agile on rocks and very friendly but tend to show increasing independence after two years of age. Weak pasterns occur in some bloodlines in barn potatoes (dairy herds), but seldom affect an exercised wether. They train easily and are very in tune to the people with whom they work. Some resemble sheepdogs in their attentiveness, watching for slight movements or gestures, looking to see what they can do for you next, even making eye contact with humans—traits not as common in other breeds. Their animal brightness is superior. In the woods, the Alpine becomes a wild animal, always watching for predators or a newly fallen tree in the trail. Docile and friendly, yes, but the instincts are running at

An Alpine wether demonstrating the Flehman Response.

high gear just below the surface. Let a coyote howl and an Alpine will stop the pack train to lift his head high and look (unless the Togg does it first). They commonly use the "Flehman Response" (curling the upper lip) in new surroundings to test the air for curious chemical clues. This behavior is a sensing mechanism practiced by many animals and thought by scientists to be connected with the vomero-nasal organ (or Jacobsen's organ), a chemical sensor located in the bony tissue of the roof of the mouth.

Don't ever offend your Alpine wether—he can be a sensitive, high-strung fellow after about age three. Of course, this isn't true of all Alpines, but of many it is. Alpines tend to be affectionate with people (when they're in the mood to be affectionate) and detest being left behind. They are very community-minded with other goats and frequently butt heads with others of their kind (the ritual reestablishment of the pecking order).

Properly treated in kidhood, an Alpine will form a strong bond with people. An older, experienced Alpine can be surprisingly trailwise, remembering the exact lay of a trail it's been on before, even when the trail is covered by a foot of snow, or remembering significant details about a route off the trail. Many a time I've used an Alpine to find the route in a pea-soup fog too dense for me to navigate. Any experienced goat can develop this sense, but Alpines seem to be the most adept at it. All these—the trailwiseness; surefootedness; strong, tight social behavior; horn-butting;

Oberhasli. *Photograph courtesy of John and Laura Peters*

and even the dark color patterns—are traits of the wild chamois. I've seen some Alpines that are colored almost exactly like one alpine variety of Swiss chamois and that even include the same extra set of teats found in wild chamois and other goat-antelopes, but not in true goats.

Oberhasli

Sometimes called "Swiss Alpines" in the past, these goats were selectively bred for color and markings—reddish brown with black dorsal stripe, facial stripe or mask, and leg stockings—and are close relatives of the French Alpine breed. The similarity between the Oberhasli and the wild Italian chamois is remarkable. Physically, Obers are very similar to Alpines, except of course for their characteristic color, and even then both tend to have a black border around the edge of the ear—yet another characteristic of the wild chamois. One undesirable physical difference for the dairy breeder happens to be desirable for the goat-packer. It's called "hockiness," a tendency for the hocks of the hind legs to be turned inward. This makes a goat more agile on rocks, but obviously leaves less room for a large, pendulous udder. A hocky goat can bound up the side of a near-vertical cliff (as opposed to a hockey player, who is agile only on ice, no puck intended). Wild caprids (goats and sheep) that live in precipitous and rocky habitats are hocky. As far as the serious goat-packer is

LaMancha.

concerned, the hocky tendency in the Oberhasli is a fortunate throwback to the natural form of the wild goat. However, hocks that rub together when walking are definitely not desirable. The sores that result cause the goat to walk in an unnatural manner to avoid the pain, eventually necessitating frequent visits to the chiropractor (and goat chiropractors are extremely hard to find).

Many Obers seem to be aquaphilic—they like water. This can be a definite advantage since most goats have to be trained to cross streams due to their natural fear of water. Obers have a pleasant, mellow, easygoing personality, and although most of them have been quite small in the past, more recently breeders have been turning out some 250-pound wethers— real beauties!

LaMancha

This is an exciting Spanish breed, commonly known as "the earless goat." Actually they have ears and can hear quite well. The external, visible part of the ear is like a little tuft with no cartilage. LaManchas come in about any color you like. Horns are black and small, resembling both the Alpine and Nubian breeds.

LaManchas are generally small goats, but some large ones can be found.

Nubian.

Crosses with larger goats of other breeds look very encouraging, though these hybrids are still experimental as working goats. In my opinion, LaManchas have the most consistently lovable and agreeable personality of all the breeds. My experience is limited to just a few animals, but the potential is there. Bonding with humans seems to be exceptional. LaManchas will follow you anywhere and therefore are a little easier to train. They are probably the most intelligent breed. You have to experience the LaMancha to fully appreciate him.

Nubian

This is the well-known goat of the floppy-eared persuasion. The enormous, pendulous ears (remnant of a desert heritage—used by many indigenous desert animals to dissipate excess body heat) and the Roman nose are the most noticeable characteristics. Nubians occur in all colors. The Nubian is the most common dairy breed in the United States. The breed was assembled in England over a hundred years ago from a collection of Indian, Near Eastern, and Mediterranean domestic goats. The size ranges from small to large, and there are small dark horns. Some bloodlines are among the largest of goats, stoutly built, and very friendly with people. Nubians are famous for their high milk production and the high butterfat content of their milk. They are also famous for lying down in the trail when you want them to go.

So here we have an animal of exceptional physiognomy whose disposition often renders him virtually useless. As a breed, Nubians often don't like to work. You can call this laziness if you like. In addition, many tend to be noisy on the trail, at camp, and at home. Nothing is more irritating than a screaming goat in the pristine wilderness. On the plus side, some can be trained as watch goats to signal when intruders come into camp but, personally, I'd rather have the intruders.

Having said that (and thoroughly offended the Nubian breeders of America) I will proffer Rule Number One of Goat-Packing (and life on planet Earth): For every rule, there is an exception. In this case, the exception is a large, 200-pound plus, Nubian named Casper (the Friendly Goat). He's a wonderful, good-looking, well-built, sturdy animal who likes people, packs beautifully, and doesn't make noise (most of the time). Casper is not the least bit lazy. He can pack 50 pounds all day with no problems. So, some Nubians can pack. In my experience, maybe ten percent of them. The question is, is it worth putting in the energy to raise and train an animal when it may be a year before you really know whether he'll work? If you already have Nubians, maybe. If you don't, the odds in favor of it are pretty low. Someday I suspect someone will come up with a Nubian line that consistently produces good pack wethers. Until then it's safer to use other breeds.

As pack-goat breeders become more numerous, there will undoubtedly be improvements in goat conformation and size, and possibly in disposition, but right now excellent animals *are* available, albeit in limited numbers. Some pack-goat breeders are primarily in the business of turning out dairy goats, so don't forget the local Dairy Goat Association as a source of pack goats. Stick with reputable breeders.

Don't forget that crossbreeds can often yield some of the best working animals by combining traits and adding a little hybrid vigor. Some of my favorite crosses are: Saanen/Togg, Alpine/Togg, Alpine/LaMancha, Togg/Ober.

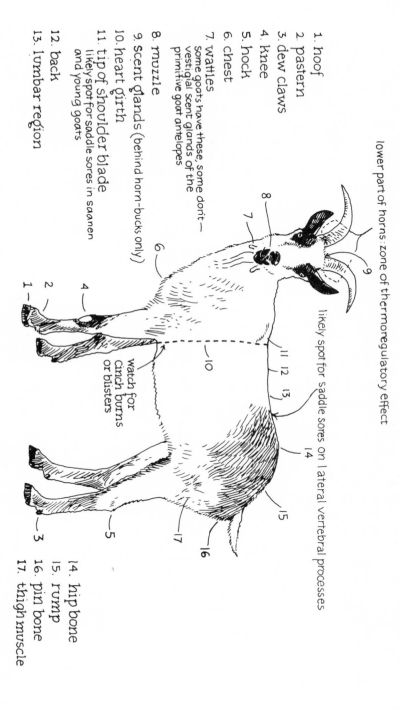

lower part of horns: zone of thermoregulatory effect

likely spot for saddle sores on lateral vertebral processes

watch for cinch burns or blisters

1. hoof
2. pastern
3. dew claws
4. knee
5. hock
6. chest
7. wattles
   some goats have these, some don't—
   vestigial scent glands of the
   primitive goat antelopes
8. muzzle
9. scent glands (behind horn-bucks only)
10. heart girth
11. tip of shoulder blade
    likely spot for saddle sores in saanen
    and young goats
12. back
13. lumbar region

14. hip bone
15. rump
16. pin bone
17. thigh muscle

■3■

Goat Hairs in My Couscous (Life on the Trail)

STARING DOWN from atop a saddle horse, the unshaven face glares at the goats, somewhat askance. The nearly subaudible tones emerging from under the shadow of the big hat have always seemed to sound something like, "Ahh, shi'!" as in, "a shilling for your thoughts"! This is followed by the more audible spitting of tobacco and a yank on a lead rope that is connected to at least eighteen overloaded pack horses. All in all, a quiet, mellow experience. In fact, the noisiest aspect of the whole encounter is produced by some of the horses as they pass by us on the trail.

This scenario was more common in the early days of goat-packing, when I first started bringing my pack strings into the mountains—territory then dominated by the hardy horse-packer with his band of Eocene remnants. Little did those packers suspect that while their progenitors walked the forests of Europe as bands of roving barbarians, the lowly herbivorous critter behind me may long before have been the original beast of burden in mountains higher than these, leading the way for other species to follow in the hands of the original packers. (It is reasonable to assume that, prior to the domestication of the horse, early goat herders loaded supplies on the backs of their goats and allowed them to follow along to markets in faraway villages. This is still practiced in Tibet.)

38

Admittedly, it had been only a year since I had been riding on high, holding on to the reins of a remnant of a past age. Had I seen a goat-pack string at that time, I think my efforts would have been directed toward struggling to stay in the saddle against the forces of uncontrolled giggling. Yes, at first the sight does seem ludicrous. But it serves to unveil the prejudice of preconception. The horse-packers of today are much more tolerant, though still a bit on the conservative side of things.

If you're going to be a real goat-packer, you'll have to be prepared for a variety of reactions, so as to maintain your composure. Laughing at someone you've never met is poor wilderness etiquette. I've selected a few of the most commonly encountered spontaneities so you can be ready for them when you bring your goats to the trailhead:

"What in the hell . . . !?"
"Now I've seen it all!"
"I don't believe it!!" (By far the most frequent udderance, pun intended.)
"Oh, how neat! I always wanted to see llamas packing!"
"What are them things?" (In a loud, coarse voice.)
"I didn't know llamas could have horns!" (Timidly.)
"Are those g-g-goats?"
"You gotta be kiddin'!" (Repugnantly, and with no eye contact.)
"Are those yaks?"
"Oh, how cute! Look, Mom . . . uh . . . what are they?"

On one unforgettable occasion I was walking up a trail with a large, fully loaded wether named Alpi walking freely behind me. A lone woman hiker, coming down the trail from the opposite direction, approached with ever-widening eyes and a look of impending Apocalypse. She glanced behind me as she fearfully stepped off her side of the trail and exclaimed, "Did you know there's a *big* goat behind you!?" Well, that one was a little more than I could resist, so I looked around and gasped, "Oh, my GOD!" and broke into a run. Alpi, of course, faithfully trotted behind as we disappeared into the trees. Trying to pack goats without a sense of humor is a terrible waste of opportunity.

Always be prepared for the nonverbal stare. It happens more often than you'd think. This encounter occurred in the northern Wind River Mountains in Wyoming. Two friends and I were walking up a washed-out road with seven goats, headed for the high country, when two red, four-wheeled all-terrain vehicles (ATVs) came screaming down the mountain and veered off the road in a cloud of dust to let our pack string go by. The two boys who piloted the machines turned off their engines and stared at the animals intently with mouths open wide. As we quietly walked by, Will, who was directly behind me, broke the ice by pointing back at the pack string, smiling, and saying, "The original ATVs." The boys neither smiled nor closed their mouths. A hundred yards up the trail, we looked behind us. The boys were still on their machines, twisted around, staring at the pack train, mouths agape.

Making progress against the endless inquisitive hordes is probably the greatest obstacle to successful goat-packing. Hikers almost always want to stop and ask questions, the same questions over and over again, every half-mile. It's a good thing goats are such good off-trail animals. You have to get off the trail to get anywhere!

One wilderness ranger, lumbering under a huge backpack, accosted me once on the Middle Fork trail in the Wind River Mountains. He was an amiable, rational fellow who, for about twenty minutes, asked very cogent questions, but the unspoken words (the emotive parts of his discourse) were: "Hey, this is supposed to be a free country, and I've been slaving under this heavy pack all summer while this *!*!* goatherder isn't carrying anything but his *!*!* sandwich! It ain't fair!"

And it wasn't fair. I was packing supplies for a group, and he was the fourth person I'd run into that morning. I was already running an hour late. It can be frustrating! So now I carry one-page information sheets I can pass out on the trail in order to gracefully escape a little more quickly. Any time unavoidably lost to trail gab I chalk up to advertising—it's better than having people think that all goat-packers are perpetually in a hurry. Besides, it saves a lot of money. When I want to do some advertising, I just saddle up and go for a walk in the mountains for a few days. (I'd rather be on the Middle Fork trail than Madison Avenue, anyway.)

Packing Up: Equipment

If you're a competent packer of any other pack animal, you can pack a goat with just a few hints here and there; the rules and equipment are basically the same. But if you've never packed an animal, pay close attention to this chapter. And don't forget—experience is the best teacher, but a little guidance saves a lot of time . . . and trouble.

Packing a goat is easy—it's like driving a car. That is, now that you know how to do it, it's easy, but if you sat behind the wheel and took off without any instruction, you could sure do a bunch of damage to a good vehicle. You can just as easily damage an animal, even permanently, with a simple mistake. Once you're a veteran goat wrangler these mistakes are very unlikely, but as a novice be very careful and always double-check the following items if you're uncertain.

Let's go through the equipment list first and make sure you've got everything you need.

A goat pack saddle is usually what's called a *sawbuck* or *crossbuck* style, but other styles, like the *decker* or *pack pad,* will work too. Most of the sawbuck goat saddles are made of two side boards called *bars,* and two wooden crossbucks that hold the bars together rigidly. A folding, or collapsing, buck is sometimes used, but I prefer the rigid one. Attached to this wood or metal frame, called a *tree,* are leather or nylon-webbing straps that are adjustable to fit the goat. The *cinch straps* buckle onto the *cinch,* which is a wide cloth strap that anchors the saddletree to the goat by being tightened around the goat's girth, just behind the front legs. The *breast collar* wraps around the breast ahead of the shoulders, and the *rump strap* goes around the rump about halfway between the tail and the hocks.

Some homemade saddles look superficially like this, but often have design flaws that can be devastating. The angle of the tree should be eighty-five to eighty-seven degrees. A ninety-degree angle, which is easier to build, will not distribute weight but will put excessive pressure on the goat's vertebral processes (the side wings on the vertebrae) and eventually cause debilitating sores. Sharper angles will hurt the ribs and constrict breathing. The inside surfaces of the bars should be beveled on top and bottom for a better fit and to compensate for wider or narrower backs. An overall tree length of 12 inches fits most goats of packable size (150 to 300 pounds).

The crossbucks themselves should be made of a hardwood (oak is best), because they are the support structure for the whole saddle and are

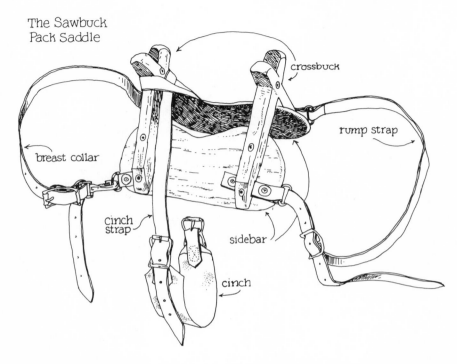

The Sawbuck
Pack Saddle

crossbuck

rump strap

breast collar

cinch
strap

sidebar

cinch

prone to being scraped by limbs and overhanging rocks. Furthermore, if saddles are thrown around in camp and vehicles, which happens sooner or later, the crossbucks will be the first to break if softer woods were used. Well-built saddles that will last a lifetime are available.

Ideally, straps should be made of latigo (or soft-strap) leather. Harness leather (used on horse pack saddles) is a hard leather and is fine for horses, but goats have a more tender hide requiring softer material. Nylon webbing works but has no give to it and, especially when it is new, can sometimes cause abrasive sores where it rubs under pressure, especially common where there are burred buckle holes.

The saddle pad (or blanket) protects the goat's back from the pressure of the saddle. The right kind of pad is critical—more so with goats than with other animals—because goats are bonier and become sore more easily. The pad should be at least 18 by 20 inches, and 1/2 to 1 inch thick. It should also be porous enough to breathe well, because goats radiate more heat than other pack animals, and an overheated goat will tire more easily. Goat-saddle pads can be made from good, porous horse pads cut down to the right size. Watch that the pad doesn't buckle and produce high

points against the goat's body. The pad's job is to distribute weight—not to concentrate it!

Panniers, or pack bags, hang from the crossbucks by loops. They should be made of durable material like canvas or nylon (Cordura, for example) because this is the part of the pack that rubs, scrapes, and bangs against the outside world, and if you like rough country your panniers will take a lot of abuse.

A *top load* is what sits on top of the saddletree and panniers, between the bucks. The top load can be in a stuff-sack or duffle, or it can be improvised. Often this top load is a sleeping bag or clothing bag.

The pack cover, sometimes called a *manty,* is a waterproof tarp (usually canvas) that covers the top of your load and ties to D-rings on the bottom corners of the panniers.

A neck collar works well as a means of control. You can hold on to your animal by the collar or attach a lead rope to the D-ring on the collar. A halter can be used in place of a collar. It's mostly a matter of personal preference, but a stubborn goat is usually more easily controlled with a halter. Latigo leather or nylon halters with D-rings work well.

The lead rope is your lifeline to your goat if he needs your help. For instance, if he's swept down the rapids on a tough river crossing, you can save him with a good lead. The rope can be soft nylon or hemp and should be at least 4 feet long. It should have a snap on the goat end to attach to the D-ring of the collar, and a loop for your hand on the other end.

A small veterinary kit is a must for any trips longer than a day. You may never need it, but if the day comes when you do way back in the tules, you'll hate yourself if you don't have one. A basic vet kit should contain: arnica liniment for sore muscles (in goats and people), saddle sores, and pain relief in injuries where the skin is not broken; an antibiotic salve or Bag Balm (a soothing antibiotic ointment available in feed stores and some drugstores); an antibiotic spray, such as gentian violet; Genticin ointment for eye inflammation; bandaging material and adhesive tape. Sterile suture needles and thread are optional.

Just one more thing in the way of equipment. Always make sure you have a pocket or belt knife on you—not in a goat pannier—but on *you!* And make sure it's sharp! Whether you're leading a pack string or just one animal, no matter what animal it is, anything can happen in the wilderness, and sometimes your animal is going to respond instinctively. His instincts are genetically programmed, and there's nothing in his genes about a pack on his back. He can get in a real jackpot before you know what happened, and in a matter of life or death you may need to cut a strap or a rope before your buddy strangles or drowns. I hope this is one thing you never have to use. There are a million other uses for a knife on the pack trail—like cutting cheese—and once you get in the habit of carrying a knife, you'll wonder how you ever did without it!

Packing Up: The Goat

The procedure for packing your goat will become routine after a while, but in the beginning it is fairly important to follow a step-by-step method that will start you off with some good habits. Your goal, of course, will be to follow this sequence faithfully so that you'll have a foolproof system of assuring that if anything goes haywire down the trail, you'll be able to lay the blame completely on the goat. This saves a good deal of embarrassment and uses one of the goat's most historically revered attributes —being a "scape goat."

There are several things to do before you actually put the saddle on the goat. We'll assume you've already made sure that you have a good animal for the job (a topic we'll discuss in more detail later).

First, talk to your goat in calm, friendly tones to let him know you're a good person and all's right with the world. As you do this, snap the lead rope to his collar and lead him over to the place where you'll pack him. A lead rope works best because some goats don't like being led by the collar alone, and although he'll most likely follow you over there even if you don't lead him, it's good to keep him accustomed to a lead rope while he's working (for reasons we'll see later). Affix the rope to a tree, post, or innocent bystander (and there are usually a few of those around a trailhead when you start unloading goats from your vehicle). It may not be necessary to tie him if you know your goat and he's the type that will stand in one place when he figures out that he's being packed. This is something goats can be trained to do, but most pick it up with experience. Bring all your equipment and lay it in a pile on the ground.

At this stage, you should already have the panniers packed, and it's critically important that the pair is balanced. If they're balanced within a pound or two of each other, you'll make things a lot easier for yourself. At first you may want to use a scale until you get the knack. In time, you'll be able to guess it within 2 pounds. If one pannier weighs 25 pounds, the other should weigh between 23 and 27 pounds. It's a good idea, if you're carrying water, to use two, or even four, containers: As you go down the trail you may notice the load listing to one side. When you get thirsty, you can do some fine-tuning of the load by drinking the ballast from the heavy side. (Make sure you pack the water bottles on top of the panniers, within easy reach.) This method of balancing shows a little more sophistication than the more Neanderthal approach of adding a rock to the light side, although both are approved methods.

Of course, use common sense, as you would with any other type of packing. For instance, don't put the leaky can of stove fuel on top of the onion bagels, and try not to put the crushable yogurt containers in the bottom of a 25-pound pannier.

Now you can begin packing your goat.

1. First grab your saddle pad and approach your goat from his left side calmly and without sudden movements, making sure you don't let the wind blow the pad in his face. If you don't know the animal personally, be careful not to make him suspicious right off. But if he's a seasoned packer you know, you can be more abrupt with your actions. (Goats don't spook as easily as horses.) Before placing the pad on his back, show it to him and let him smell it. Then hold his collar (if you don't know him) to show him you are in control.

Put the pad on his back considerably forward of where it will eventually sit, and slowly pull it back until the front edge of the pad is over his shoulders. The pad should be well centered on his back now. If you get it too far back, lift it up and set it down forward of the shoulders and pull it back once again. Don't try to pull the pad forward to adjust it because this will go against the natural direction of hair growth and cause lumps of backward-pressed hair that will make the goat uncomfortable and cause sores. If this was his first time being saddled by you, congratulate him. Goats like being talked to while being saddled—it's reassuring to them.

2. Now grab the saddle by the front crossbuck and let him smell it (if he's new to the game). Set it down on the pad just behind the protruding part of the shoulder blade. If your goat has flat shoulders, this won't be so critical. Outflared shoulder blades, more common in some Saanens, but occasionally occurring in any breed, can be a place for saddle sores to develop if the saddle is too far forward. When properly fitted, the saddle should appear a bit forward of the middle of the back. Check that no straps are caught under the saddle.

3. Now, working from the left side of the goat again, as always, reach under the rib cage and grab the cinch, which should be dangling on the right side just behind the front legs. (If it's not there, you may have put the saddle on backward. If so, quickly look around to make certain no one is watching, and swap ends on the saddle. If someone is watching, you may want to point out the presence of a rare arboreal bird in the tree just behind him before turning the saddle around. A quick command of impressive-sounding Latin bird names can be handy at critical moments such as this.)

Buckle the cinch to the cinch strap on the left side of the saddle and tighten it up (with about 8 to 10 pounds of pull). Check pressure by slipping two fingers between the cinch and the goat. It should take some effort to do this. At this point, a secure cinch is not absolutely essential, because a seasoned pack goat will bloat himself with air in anticipation of your cinching him so that the cinch will loosen when you're finished. For this reason, you must always check and retighten the cinch again after packing is finished and then again a quarter-mile or so up the trail. *More wrecks and saddle sores are caused by loose cinches than by any other factor!*

4. Now you're ready to buckle down the breast collar so that it lays snugly, but not tight, around the shoulders. Too loose is better than too tight. It will be in use only when the goat is climbing hills, jumping, or pulling in a string.

5. Next, drop the rump strap over the rump and take out the slack (do not tighten this one, either). It should rest about halfway between the pinbones and the hocks (just below the tip of the tail). The adjustment is usually on a *conway buckle,* which is adjusted once for a given animal and stays there unless he grows or the leather gets water-soaked and stretches. If your wether flinches his hind legs or hops with his hind legs or walks holding his rump down, you probably got the rump strap too tight. So, first-time wranglers and/or wranglers with first-time goats should walk the goat around at this stage to see that everything looks right.

6. You can put the panniers on now. Just drape the loops of each pannier over the crossbuck on the opposite side of the saddle. With heavy loads it's best, but not essential, to do both panniers at the same time. Some panniers come with adjustable loops, but these should be let out only for very bulky loads like 5-gallon water cans or the larger accordions. The loaded panniers should hang more or less vertically along the sides of the goat. If they stick out like wings, well, you'll be hitting rocks and trees and pedestrians, not to mention making the load unstable (wobbly). This can tire your goat and even give him saddle sores. Extend the loops until the panniers hang vertically.

7. The top load, if you have one, goes on next. It's better, of course, to get all the cargo in the panniers if you can, to keep the center of gravity lower and your overhead clearance reduced, but sawbuck saddles are designed for top bags. Make sure that the top load is lighter than *one* loaded pannier. A sleeping bag or clothing bag is customary.

Place the bag perpendicular to the topline of the goat, between the crossbucks. A long stuff-sack or duffle should lie over the top of the panniers and not stick out too much beyond the panniers on the sides. Press it down into the saddle and secure it, using top-load straps (nylon webbing), stock equipment on most panniers. These are usually fastened with quick-release buckles for quick and easy unpacking or for emergencies when the pack must come off pronto. Nylon cord or, better still, bungee cords can be used in lieu of top-load straps for securing the top load to the crossbucks. A cross strap spans the distance between the two top-load straps and should cross the duffle in about the middle. Check that the top bag is still centered on top—not so much visually as by weight and balance.

8. For extra protection, or on rainy-looking days, you can tie a canvas pack cover over the entire load, tying off to the D-rings at the bottom of the panniers.

Now, step back and take a look. That's all there is to it. If you were packing a horse, you'd still be tightening up the latigo on the saddle. Once you're practiced, all this should take about sixty seconds or so. Three goats would still pack more quickly than one horse.

One thing to do after you've packed the animal but before you take off, is to check and secure the load one more time. Before retightening the cinch, place your hand on the lefthand side of the load (remember, you're still standing on the left side of the goat) and push down sharply (about 4 to 6 inches). Let the load rock back into position. If it tends to drop lower on one side when it's rocking, you know that side is heavy, so adjust the weight accordingly. Then check the cinch by lifting the left pannier. There's a good chance (especially with an older goat) that you'll need to pull the cinch strap up another notch.

Before we head up the trail, let's look at some less-frequently used packing techniques.

Horse-packers generally use rope hitches of one sort or another to stabilize the pack load and secure it to the horse after putting on the pack cover. I used a diamond or a double-diamond hitch or, rarely, a basket hitch, virtually every time I packed a horse with soft-canvas panniers. In twenty years of packing goats, I've never found a need to throw a diamond hitch of any kind. It just isn't necessary. Goats are smooth walkers and rarely need the extra security. However, I have found two "sling" hitches used in traditional horse-packing—the barrel hitch and the basket hitch—to be useful on goats for very specialized loads.

A hitch is simply a way of wrapping a rope around a load so it won't come off until you want it to. Some barrel hitches are designed to secure loads that are carried lengthwise along both sides of the animal but that

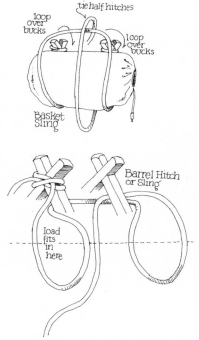

are not small enough or otherwise appropriate for a set of panniers—such as fence posts, long pieces of firewood, large duffles, and, yes, barrels. Essentially, a barrel hitch is two loops of rope (or nylon webbing) suspended off the saddlebucks, inside of which you sling your load, balanced of course, on both sides. Beyond this, you can be creative. If you have D-rings in your cinch, you can bring the free end of the lash rope down through one of the D-rings, back up and over the load and down the other side through the other D-ring. Then tie it off on the lash rope or back up on the buck. This suspends the load by gravity as well as clasping it tightly against the animal. A basket hitch can also be used for this purpose.

For short jaunts like hauling firewood to camp in the desert, a gravity suspension is all you need. In that case, you just hang the wood in the loops of the sling and tie it off up top. A quicker method is simply to have two ropes each about 10 feet long and dally them midway around the bucks. Bring the ropes underneath and over your two bundles of wood and tie off the loose ends to the bucks. A third load can then be bundled up on top and tied around the middle to the bucks, the ends resting on the side bundles. Bundles can be up to 5 feet long.

Barrel hitches are a good method of packing long, heavy sleeping bags. Three, five, or seven sleeping bags fit into nice configurations for a top-loaded barrel hitch.

There are two ways to "manty up" a load by using tarps. You can use two waterproof tarps (about 5 to 6 feet square). Wrap these around your supplies, especially if you have loads like plant presses, loose rock specimens, or grain sacks. Of course, the two wrapped loads must be balanced. Then suspend these individually wrapped parcels from the bucks. If you are good at it, and careful, you can have a waterproof package even when it's submerged on river crossings.

The other way to manty up a goat is to use one large tarp (8 or 10 feet square). Some ground cloths work for this. Wrap the entire load into one roll about 16 inches in diameter and tie it with a rope. This is lashed

to the saddle with a basket hitch. No panniers are needed. This technique works well for any awkward load that can be rolled up. A 10-foot inflatable rubber raft, for instance, carries well when rolled up and draped over the saddle and basket-hitched to the goat. For some loads, mantying-up has real advantages, but most of the time panniers are much handier and quicker.

A "jumping goat hitch" is a very simple method of keeping it all together on trails where the goat will be doing a lot of jumping. It's just a rope snapped into the D-ring on the cinch and brought over the load and tied off on the other D-ring. It simply keeps the panniers from flying up when the goat jumps over rocks on scree fields or hops streams, and it keeps panniers from floating when the goat swims rivers.

Well, that goat's been tied up too long. Let's get going up the trail and see what happens.

Life on the Trail

There are two ways to start up the trail with your goat(s): on the lead or free. If you're in an area where you can hike legally without leading your goat, you'll have the pleasure of the freedom of unburdened hiking (without even a lead rope to hang on to) with a companion who just tags along because he enjoys your company. The choice depends, at least partially, on whether you're actually on a trail or not. If you're out in an open field or desert country, your little friend can walk free, alongside or behind you. I prefer hiking this way whenever possible. This is also the preferred method on forest trails, but there are several factors we need to discuss that may put restrictions on your freedom.

Number one is ferocious predators. The world is teeming with deadly ferocious predators. It's hard to escape their watchful eye, and they're in the habit of attacking when you least expect it. Unfortunately, their owners think of them as harmless puppy dogs and do very little to restrain them. I'm not speaking of the responsible dog owners who are considerate of other people as well as their dogs, but of those few who choose to close their eyes to their dogs' predatory instincts and/or neglect to train their lovable canines and then release them into the world unrestrained and unwatched. A dog will attack a goat under the right circumstances—principally when the goat is running or just seems to be running. Most goats, by instinct, will jump up on a high point when frightened. If there's no high point nearby, a goat will typically start, then run a few feet or a few yards and stop and stare. Those few feet or few yards can be all it takes for a dog to latch on to your goat. If your goat has horns, he may assume a defensive posture with horns tilted forward. A goat with horns can defend himself and even disembowel a persistent dog. I've seen it happen with my own goats. But a dog can also injure or kill your animal, especially a young one. I've had to endure that, also. People can and do bond with goats just as closely as they do with dogs or other pets; to lose one is a serious matter. In either case, vicious canine-caprid encounters on the trail are unpleasant, no matter who wins, and they can usually be avoided. Dogs could be restrained, which seems the natural way to avert the problem, considering that the dog is usually the aggressor. But since some dog owners adamantly refuse to restrain their pets regardless of the consequences, even where federal and state leash laws exist, the burden falls on you. Most dog attacks can be deterred by keeping the goat on a short lead. Keep him close to your body so he doesn't appear to be moving away from the attack, and generally nothing will happen but a lot of annoying barking.

If you're not leading your goat (holding on to the lead rope), always have the lead rope attached to his collar and wrapped around the front buck or tucked under a cross strap where you can get at it quickly. There are times when you may need to gain control of him quickly, so just get in the habit of keeping that lead handy. Now that I've scared you a little, I can tell you that most dog-goat encounters are pretty peaceful, but for your animal's sake you should always be ready. I've lost fourteen goats out of several hundred to dogs over the years, and it's never easy to deal with. My losses were all in my home pasture, however, and not on the trail.

Another instance where you don't want your goat to walk free is where the law forbids it. On some public lands, state or federal (such as U.S. Forest Service trails), pack animals must be led. These laws originally pertained to horses and now apply to any pack animal—including goats. You need to check with the local manager of the area you'll be using to be sure, because there may be separate district-level regulations or interpretations. These rules are generally easy to comply with, being designed primarily to make sure a person has control of his animals on the trail for the protection of other backcountry users, the animals themselves, and the environment. This last consideration applies especially to switchbacks on steep hills, which most animals will try to shortcut. "Cutting" switchbacks causes erosion, raises taxes, and is illegal—need any more reasons? Goats can be trained not to cut switchbacks, but you may still be legally required to lead them. Keep that goat on the trail (unless, of course, you're not on the trail to begin with).

After several days of walking free, it is easy to slip into complacency. Ambling along, basking in the wonders of the wilderness, doing what we all end up doing while hiking up the trail—seeing, hearing, feeling, tasting, smelling, and awaiting new sensations around the next bend—you can become oblivious to whether your faithful companion, who's doing all the work, is still behind you. A goat whose gear is snagged on a stub generally bleats to get your attention, because being separated from his companions is a source of great distress to him. But I've had more than one pack goat who made not a sound when separated. Considering that goats are virtually soundless pack animals—unlike horses, whose hooves can be clearly heard—it's almost impossible to know if your buddy's dropped off, unlikely as that may be, unless you turn around and check. For this reason, it is sensible to have a plan; either get in the habit of looking around and checking regularly, or carry little quick-fastening tinklebells that can be attached to the collar. Some folks like to do this anyway in bear country to avoid accidental run-ins.

I can remember one unfortunate incident where a woman rented a goat named Alfonse from me and took off for the hills. I'd acquired Alfonse after he was grown, but he seemed to pack well except for a couple of quirks. Mainly, he didn't like other goats. In a pack string, he'd constantly fight and throw tantrums of jealous rage. By himself, he seemed okay, although a bit snooty. Well, Alfonse was raised with horses, thoroughbreds to be precise, and he thought he was one. (It's a common practice to keep goats with horses, especially thoroughbred racehorses, for two reasons. First, the goat has a calming effect on high-strung, spirited horses. It was, I'm told, common for horse trainers to keep one special goat with a favorite racehorse. The night before a race, this goat would actually stay in the stall with the horse, which would help him to rest well before the race. Occasionally an unscrupulous competitor would hire someone to steal the goat in the night, which would unsettle the horse so much that he would invariably perform poorly the next day. From this practice, we have inherited the cliché, "Don't let 'em get yer goat"! Second, many horse breeders believe that the goat's immunity to distemper is somehow passed on to the horse. I know quite a few horse breeders who will swear that this phenomenon is well borne out in practice with their own animals, in spite of the official veterinary position that it is as yet unproven.)

Anyway, Alfonse was also raised around people, so he showed some human bonding, but he had actually spent more time with horses. Well, somewhere down the trail on the first day, this poor woman turned around to check on Alfonse and he was gone! In time she spotted him way up on a ridge, following a group of elk who were headed south. It started to rain about then, and Alfonse had her raincoat, and she couldn't catch him. He apparently thought the elk were horses. Well, at some point he either got tired of the chase or got close enough to notice that the "horses" just didn't smell quite right, because he showed up at the trailhead later that day, as did his soggy hiking companion. Since this was the second time he'd pulled this stunt, ol' Alfonse went into early retirement. He's back with his own kind now, living on a thoroughbred ranch somewhere in Wyoming.

The moral? Bonding and early training are critically important if you want a faithful companion. Moral number two: If there's any question about the goat's loyalty, use a lead rope or a bell.

There are other circumstances where you may have to use the lead rope. Most goats, even when trained to cross streams early in life, will still hesitate when faced with the prospect of getting their feet wet. Grabbing the lead rope is often enough encouragement. With goats not trained until later in life, you may have to pull on the lead rope to get results. Some goats, who have had particularly bad experiences at water crossings, can require some heavy-duty pulling. Goats are strong animals, so avoid creating unnecessarily stressful occurrences while walking streams, or especially wading or swimming rivers. Speak in reassuring tones and be gentle but persistent. Goats are good swimmers but for the most part don't enjoy water. Some Oberhaslis seem to enjoy standing in water, and even swimming, but that's aberrant behavior for most other breeds.

On stream crossings, most goats prefer to walk on rocks, or jump from rock to rock, or jump the entire stream if it's a short enough span. Any of these behaviors is perfectly acceptable. You should let them find their own way whenever possible. If a goat freaks out when he sees water and tries to run away, he's got a serious hangup and needs to see a counselor— that is, a goat trainer, and maybe you (see Chapter 10).

Sometimes a goat will lie down in the trail. If this happens, there are several things that can be wrong.

1. Grab the tip of the goat's ear between your thumb and index finger and gently lift it until it's pointed straight up—then suddenly let go. If the ear falls down like a limp dishrag along the side of the head, you have a Nubian. Many Nubians love to lie down in the trail. It's part of their genetic makeup and inherent abhorrence of work!

As I've said before, there are some exceptions to this rule, but one of the most common letter exchanges I have with people goes like this:

Dear John: My goat won't pack. Signed, A Frustrated Goat-Packer.
Dear Frustrated: Does your goat have floppy ears?
Dear John: Yes, my goat has floppy ears. Signed, Desperately Wanting
to Pack Goats.
Dear Desperate: I thought so. You need a new goat.

I would love to be able to say that Nubians can be trained out of this mindset, but that hasn't been my experience. Once in a while a goat of the floppy-eared persuasion will work and not lie down. These go on to be superlative pack animals, but this is so rare as to seem to be almost a genetic defect in the breed. I truly hope that someday someone finds a bloodline of the Nubian that packs well, because they tend to have a superior bone structure and size.

2. Sometimes a goat will lie down because of sores. Check for chafing, swelling, upturned- or worn-hair spots, or just warm spots on the hide under the rump strap or under the saddletree at the shoulders or upper lumbar region of the back. Watch your goat—he will often turn his head around and look directly at the irritated area.

3. Your goat may be tired. Things causing fatigue may be: overloading; poor conformation, such as weak pasterns or a narrow chest; overheating —heavy breathing through the mouth, tongue hanging out, sweating; illness.

4. You may just have a lazy goat! If you didn't acquire your goat from a genuine pack-goat breeder or dealer, you've taken the chance of getting an untested animal. You may have gotten a real good price, but no guarantee. Beware! With a little training, anyone can pick out a structurally sound, well-built animal. But it takes considerable experience to spot a lazy one, and lazy is the same as lame when it comes to working, whether the worker be a goat, a horse, or a person.

5. Rarely, hoof wear can cause a goat to limp or lie down. The real cause for this is almost always overworking an unconditioned animal, unless there is a deformity of the hoof. An unexercised goat living in a pen with soft ground has feet that are soft, like yours if you wear shoes all day. Try taking off your shoes and backpacking up a rocky trail for six hours. You're going to sit down (and be in pain) after about the first mile. Conditioning is the next most important aspect of successful goat-packing, right after acquiring a good animal. (Conditioning will be discussed in Chapter 10.) Generally, if you have to trim your goat's hooves regularly, your goat is not properly conditioned to rocky trails. His pen or pasture should contain enough rock (one large boulder to jump on is often sufficient) to wear down the normal hoof growth. This will also toughen the hoof (so it corresponds to the sole of your hiking boot), and you'll have an intrepid hiker on rocky terrain. Walking on paved roads two or three times a week will achieve the same result.

If neither of these options is possible, longer trips in the backcountry, say six to eight miles on a weekend every two weeks, will usually accomplish the same thing, and it gives you the ideal excuse to get away. ("Oh, sorry. I can't go to your brother-in-law's slide show on his Iowa vacation this weekend. I have to exercise my goat!")

And remember, every minute you spend with your goat is reinforcing his bond with you, which makes him a better, friendlier, more serviceable animal. The best time for reinforcing bonding is on extended trips in the backcountry, or at least away from the pasture. This is when he's least secure in his surroundings and more dependent on you for security. He will learn and be more sensitive to your likes and dislikes in this environment, and you will learn his likes and dislikes and quirks. Each goat has his own personality, and you'll pick up on it more quickly on the trail.

Off the Trail

The term "on the trail" is a cliché that may be stretching it a bit with goats. Most goat-packers are inclined to wander "off the trail" because it's so much more easily done with a small surefooted pack animal who doesn't need to be led on a string. If you're inclined that way, you should work with your goat under off-trail conditions. Trees and rocks are obstacles that your animal must learn to negotiate with his pack on. He will learn where his panniers are and how much clearance he has with experience—so give it to him.

Training a goat to respond to verbal commands is not necessary for all people's needs, but if you want your goat to learn those skills, practice them every day on the trail. "Whoa" for stop, of course; "Come on" for go; "Up" for jump; and "NO!" for all sorts of things, can be handy commands when walking free. Maybe the most useful verbalization you can use is "Easy." It's not a command at all, but is used to calm your goat when an uncertain or dangerous situation is imminent, such as trees blowing over in a windstorm, dogs on the trail, or gunfire. You should try not to be nervous when you say it, or he'll think he's supposed to be nervous. You may never have to use it, but it's a good idea to be prepared to give him a reassuring word when necessary.

Goats are famous for the "poker face" look. Animals that can't outrun, but must outsmart, predators instinctively use this method of dealing with threats. A goat will always look for a high point or cliff ledge to jump on when threatened. If none is around, he most often will stand still and keep looking straight ahead, particularly when it is dark. What gives him away is the carotid artery in his neck. You should get used to noticing it throb on his lower neck. Usually his pulse rate will be around seventy to eighty beats per minute (eighteen to twenty beats every fifteen seconds). Spotting an accelerated rate, say about 110, can clue you in that he's excited and needs calming, or perhaps that he's not feeling well.

Accelerated or depressed heart rate can also be used to ascertain suspected plant poisoning. For instance, a digitalislike substance (apocynin) in plants in the dogbane family will produce virtually no symptoms except that the goat's heart rate may drop to forty to fifty, while he slows down his walking speed slightly. Too much can kill him in what looks like sleep. The good news is that in most regions goats rarely eat enough of these, or any other poisonous plants, in an area they know, unless there's nothing else to eat.

Right of Way

While packing on the trail, there are certain unwritten rules, and some written rules such as federal regulations or district-level guidelines on public lands, for packing etiquette. In any case, the intent is courtesy to others on the trail. Simply stated, the larger animal has the right of way. This would be self-evident if you met a pack elephant on the trail: Someone would have to move! The rule is not set up because bigger animals can go wherever they want simply because they are bigger. Actually, the opposite is more accurate. On a narrow trail with numerous obstacles and uncertain footing, it's the larger animal that is more vulnerable. The bigger they are, the harder they fall. Basically, it's easier for small animals to get off the trail.

If you meet a horse-packer on the trail, whether he has one horse unpacked or a loaded pack string, get off the trail at a reasonable distance, stop, and let him by. If he's gaining on you from behind, do the same. Also do the same for llama-packers. Since llama-packers are used to thinking of themselves as the little guy, they often get off the trail for goat strings out of habit, but technically the burden is on you to yield. Since the goat-packer is the "little guy" most often, it's best to get in the habit of yielding to others, unless of course you run into a string of pack ducks!

Generally, backpackers yield to animal-packers, but in some cases you may want to read the situation. For instance, if there is a troop of forty Boy Scouts bearing down on you from uptrail and you have only two goats, it's easier for you to lead your two goats off the trail and allow the downhill momentum of the hikers to proceed.

Your tendency will be to get off the trail on the uphill side, but proper etiquette is to go 10 to 20 feet downhill, especially when yielding to other pack animals. This is because the other animals will feel less intimidated looking down at you, and if they do spook, they will tend to feel safer going uphill.

The End of the Trail

On a long or difficult hike, your goat will likely want to lie down and take a break. You should let him. Goats can do this with their packs on. They are very comfortable lying down with a full load. In fact, it seems they are actually *more* comfortable, if you watch the way they lean back on their panniers. It's like sitting in a reclining chair. Since they can also

Photograph by Jeff Corney

feed comfortably with their packs on, the best policy is to let them carry their loads all day and take the load off at the final destination for the day. If, however, you decide to take a midday siesta for a few hours, it's better to take off the panniers and let the goats hang out wearing just their saddles.

When you finally do arrive at camp, unpack your goat and reward him as soon as possible. Carry a good handful of COB (rolled corn, oats, barley—no molasses) or pelletized alfalfa/grain mix in a bag in your pocket or daypack. Letting him have a treat at the end of the working day will make him happy and more goal-oriented the next day. If you're consistent with the reward, it will assure a better performance in the future and a goat that looks forward to getting to camp. In time, he will expect a reward, which, by the way, should always be accompanied by words of praise and some stroking.

If a goat begins to get aggressive about getting his reward, do not give it to him until he settles down. Let him go out and feed awhile, then offer it to him. He must learn that he'll get it, but only when you're ready to give it to him. This is one way of letting him know you're boss and also teaches patience—a real virtue for a pack goat. Some people think it's cute to have a goat beg for his reward. But this will eventually lead to aggressive behavior, and a 250-pound goat is a deceptively powerful animal who is not so cute when he's standing with his front hooves on a grown man's shoulders. (A large goat can stand on his hind legs to a height of 7-1/2 feet.) Teach patience, not aggressiveness!

If you have a pack string, you can feed each goat individually out of your hand or spread the grain or pellets out on a pack cover (3-by-4-foot canvas tarp, five goats per tarp).

There are two ways of removing the load from a goat: the slow method and the fast method. In the slow method, you peel everything off, piece by piece, in reverse order from the packing procedure, starting with the pack cover and ending with saddle and pad. This will take about one and one-half to two minutes. The fast method takes about twenty seconds and involves three steps: 1. unbuckling the cinch; 2. unbuckling or unsnapping the breast collar; and 3. grabbing each crossbuck of the saddle, lifting up and back, and moving the rump strap back and away from the rump. Don't try this if you aren't sure you can lift the combined weight of cargo and saddle. I prefer the fast method most of the time, especially since most of my packing is with strings of eight to ten animals. This unburdens the goats more quickly and can make suppertime arrive fifteen minutes sooner (a sensible goat wrangler always keeps his priorities in perspective).

Speaking of wrangling, you have a decision to make at this juncture. You can let your goat(s) go out and browse (as opposed to graze), or you can tether him (them). If you let him browse, it's a good idea to attach a bell to the D-ring on his collar. I use a small carabiner to hold the bell on, but you can use any kind of snap for speed's sake. The bell should be left on all night to keep you informed of possible ferocious predators and night monsters invisible to your own eyes. Once you tune in to your bellwether, you can determine if the sound of the bell is produced by his sudden act of alarm, scratching an itch, or attending to a physiological need.

If you decide to tether your goat overnight (which is actually required by law in some areas) you have several options. In a meadow, you can use a picket; that is, a stake in the ground to which the goat is tied by a 10- to 25-foot-long rope (1/2-inch nylon rope or 1/2-inch nylon webbing). Try this first at home, where you can watch while your goat becomes picket-broke; otherwise, he may hurt himself. If there are too many trees, you can tie him to a big tree with heavy bark that he won't eat, making sure he can't reach saplings and thin-barked trees that he may want to strip. You'll have to move him around to keep him fed, and don't let him stay there so long that he devastates a circle around the tree. This is your responsibility. (Remember, the deserts of the Middle East that were allegedly created by goats were really created by goat herders!)

If neither of these methods is practical due to various obstacles, you may want to use the overhead-line picket, also called a high-line. This is a line (1/4-inch nylon) about 5 to 6 feet off the ground, strung between two trees or two rocks, and up to 50 feet long. The loop of the lead rope slides on this line, and is connected to the goat by his neck collar. It's a very efficient technique for shrubby or brambly country. In a flat meadow, this same picket line can be laid on the ground and staked taut at each end.

No matter which type of picket you decide on, use 1/2-inch rope or webbing for any rope that's dangling or loose and that might wrap around an animal's feet or neck. Quarter-inch nylon rope will hold a goat but can cause severe rope burns and even cut off circulation in a limb if it gets wrapped around it. Half-inch rope is much less likely to cause damage.

Once a goat is picket-broke, which takes about two days in his pasture where you can watch him, he will be incredibly good about keeping himself from getting tied up in his rope. However, a smart goat will learn this much sooner than a not-so-smart one, and that's one reason that pack-goat breeders cull out the not-so-smart ones. The ability to learn quickly is very important for a working goat but is not heavily selected for by breeders of goats whose only job is to have their udders squeezed twice a day. Think about that if you're looking to buy a pack goat.

You need to allow your goat at least three hours a day for free feeding time at camp to maintain proper nutrition. Once the goat learns the schedule, he'll make good use of camp time.

Barnyard goats are famous for running for the barn at the landing of the first raindrop (true wimps at heart). But raised at least partially in the wild or on the range, goats learn to be more tolerant. In really nasty weather, they'll seek out trees, overhanging rocks, or other protection. A pack goat learns from frequent pack trips to hike right along in rain and snow and wind. He's seasoned and accepts it—another reason to train a goat young. Starting a goat on trips at the age of one month, following big goats, whom he loves to mimic, will condition him to what his ancient cousins experienced in the wild.

A barn potato who's never braved the elements will think he's going to freeze to death under the ordinary conditions accepted by a working goat. A pampered animal is also not physically conditioned, so he is more likely to become hypothermic. Goats that are worked are tough animals, like their wild progenitors, but even so, hypothermia is a possibility under the right conditions. Seasoned pack goats tolerate belly-deep snow and temperatures down to thirty degrees below zero even when sleeping out in these conditions. The situation most likely to lead to hypothermia (in goats and people) is a long, drenching rainstorm at near-freezing temperatures.

Shivering is not hypothermia. It is the body's way of trying to gain more heat, and goats do it when they're cold. Hypothermia is a critical lowering of overall body temperature to a point where body functions are impaired, and death can result. A hypothermic goat will stand or lie down, intermittently shivering, with a blank stare, drooping ears, and an expression of sadness. Goats have very expressive faces, and you can read their emotions once you get to know them. If a goat has hypothermia, the whites of his eyes may develop a bluish cast, and so will the inside of his lips. Pull down the lower lip if you suspect hypothermia, and look at any skin that normally is pink (even the gums) to check for a white color. Some goats have black lips, so the white is hard to see. If a goat has hypothermia, he's likely to hang his head and stagger, and any skin that is normally pink will have a pale, whitish appearance. The wilderness treatment for goat hypothermia is the same as for people—get into a sleeping bag with the animal. Yes, it can be done. Taking off your clothes will transmit heat more quickly. If the goat's truly hypothermic, he won't resist. Commonsense preventive measures will keep this emergency procedure from ever having to occur.

It is the goat's small body size that makes him more prone to hypothermia than, say, a horse. I know llama-packers who carry a thermometer just for the purpose of detecting hypothermia. (It might be interesting to see a person trying to crawl into a sleeping bag with a llama!) Goats have a variable rectal temperature (a desert adaptation), but normally it ranges from 102° to 103° Fahrenheit. If the goat looks hypothermic and his rectal temperature is below 85°, it is time for you to take action.

I've only seen the beginnings of hypothermia in a goat once, and it was due to a river crossing in very cold weather. The goat was a yearling without much body mass. An hour cuddled with me against a tree with warm clothing draped over us took care of it.

Goats lose heat very rapidly when their hide and hair are thoroughly soaked. This causes energy loss even if hypothermia isn't likely. To help keep their energy up, I often bring a fly (instead of a tent), which the goats and I can sleep under. A fly is a tarp, usually nylon, that can be tied down on the corners, sides, and ends. They come in all sizes and, personally, I think they are much more serviceable and versatile than tents for almost all conditions. Flies can be tied down to be a tent without a floor or mosquito netting. (By my own preference, I use flies rather than tents, even if I don't have goats with me.)

With a fly, you can store all your gear, plus sleep and let several goats sleep with you, all protected in one spot. If you prefer separate rooms, you can carry an extra tarp for the caprine contingent. A fly that is 10 feet by 10 feet will contain you, your gear, and three goats comfortably and will weigh about 6 pounds with all the stakes (less than a tent). If you have a large pack string, you can have a small fly for yourself, say eight-by-eight, and a large one, maybe ten-by-ten, for all the goats. You can train the goats as to whose fly is whose, and they'll know not to enter the wrong one

(yours has the gear in it). This makes them happy, conserves energy, and spoils them a little bit. On outings when only people have tents or flies, an envious goat may try to sneak into one, walking on tiptoe when no one is looking. This is normal, even if the weather is beautiful: He has pleasant memories of feeling secure under a strip of nylon. Don't think this is cute! Restrain him right away, or you'll have a 200-pound tent-raiding marauder (with horns) on your hands. I'd encourage providing cover for your goat in very rainy climates, but in most cases it's not really necessary—trees and rocks usually suffice.

To assure your animal's optimum tolerance for cold, keep his energy high. That means allowing him to eat until he's full. Goats seem to show a preference for woody plants when they get cold. Willows and huckleberry bushes, the dead bark of pine, spruce, and fir, and twigs of many kinds will fill the need, along with some sedges or grasses and a handful of grain a day. Working goats should be allowed at least three hours of browsing and 1/4-pound of grain a day. Goats used to the wild country will carefully select a diet that fulfills their needs.

The Morning After

Well, after a good night's sleep and a hearty bowl of cream-of-lumps, it's time to "head 'em up and move 'em out"! But where are the little buggers? Your first thought, of course, is, "I knew this goat-packing thing sounded kinda hokey from the beginning—just a way for some fella to sell a book. Aha! The Book!" So you turn to Chapter 2 of your *Goats in the Wilderness Handbook* and read: "Once bonded and a trust established, your pack goats will stay around camp at night untethered."

"Sure," you say. "I don't see any goats around this camp!"

Back to the book: "They may range out and feed early in the morning, but usually close to home and generally in sight of the camp area. Listen for those bells. They'll tinkle while the goats are feeding."

"Tinkle, schminkle—I don't hear any bells, and there ain't any goats in them willows. I knew it was a sham!"

"If they are not out browsing and not bedded down in camp, look for a high rocky point with a view, overlooking camp. Goats will often feel more secure at night on a lofty lookout post in sight of camp. They've most likely been lying there, watching you cook breakfast. *Note:* Since they are lazing there, motionless, in the morning sun, you may not hear their bells, and in panic you may have already been frantically thumbing through this handbook seeking guidance. If there are others in your party observing your panicked behavior, this may be a moment of embarrassment."

Slowly, you move your eyes up to the top of the small rock outcrop next to camp and meet the eyes of a peaceful group of lounging goats watching your every move. As you feel a flush come over your face, you shout, "Don't panic, guys! They're right up there where I thought they'd be. You know goats—always up in them rocks (whew!)!"

At this point you go to the hardware pannier (panniers organized by category are much easier to find things in—food, hardware, clothing, accordions, etc.), find the grain bell that you faithfully ring every time you feed them grain or pellets at home, and ring it. The ensuing stampede is followed by a small handful of treats for each member of your string. Sometimes in the morning they may not come to the bell right away, or at all, due to the fact that only one thing rates as high as eating on a wether's list of neat things to do—and that's basking in the morning sun. For a castrated male, this is the absolute pinnacle of goat ecstasy. There are two things you can do at this point: 1. make another attempt to scrape more of the burnt cream-of-lumps out of your bowl and try the bell a little later; or 2. climb up the hill and grab the lead goat, which the others will follow (unless their ecstasy is too intense).

Tie them up by their leads to trees for saddling. Many goats will stand around and wait to be saddled, but this is a ticklish time because goats are about as fond of being loaded down with heavy packs as people are. They may try to avoid it by staying out of reach, and this is a bad habit to let develop. So it's better to tie them up and remove the temptation.

After you've packed them up, they're ready to be tied in a string.

■4■
The Pack String

A PACK STRING (OR PACK TRAIN), no matter what animal it consists of, is a thing of beauty. Done successfully, it's a science! It is a long line of well-trained, well-conditioned animals, each more powerful than the man or woman in the lead, working together in an orderly fashion toward a common goal.

In a goat pack string it is important that the animals be strung together at the proper distance. Too long a rope between animals and a leg can get caught in a dangling loop. Too short and the hind goats will be constantly pulling back to get more clearance. On very rugged trails, the maximum length should be used. Three-and-a-half to 4-1/2 feet of rope usually works well. A 7- to 8-foot lead rope can be folded in half and used. One end snaps onto the D-ring of the collar while the other end is looped over the back buck of the saddle ahead. Don't tie onto the goat's tail, as is done with horses. On rugged trails, where wrecks are possible, and elsewhere just to be on the safe side, the rope should be attached to a *breakaway*. This is usually a leather strip or section of hemp twine about 3/16-inch in diameter tied in a loose loop around the saddle buck. It serves as a "weak link in the chain," and its function is to break. If a goat falls off a cliff (which isn't likely to happen) or one decides to walk around the wrong side of

66

a tree (which is not uncommon with young goats), it could save a lot of screaming and/or injury. Breakaways should not be used during training. The trainee must think the rope is secure to respect its power. Of course, you'll be ever watchful during the training period.

Now, for the most important part of stringing goats—the order of the string. The difference between an orderly pack string and an unruly jumble of caprid chaos is generally not the components but the *arrangement* of the components. It's the job of the goat-packer to know who's first, who's last, and the exact position of everyone in between. In some groups of equal age and size this may not be so critical. Furthermore, goats who work hard day after day have little energy left for or inclination toward dominance fighting. But in general, carefully organizing the string will add to everyone's enjoyment.

To further confuse matters, goats are herd animals with a specific pecking order. But that isn't necessarily the order they pack best in.

First and foremost, pick a good lead goat for the number-one position. If you have a female, she should be in the lead. As with mules, female goats make the best leaders. An otherwise unmanageable wad of biting, horning string-dummies can be transformed into an orderly line of majestic beasts of burden that Emily Post would be proud of if you simply install a doe as the string leader.

To understand the rationale here, let's go back to the wild goats and goat-antelopes. In the wild, goats usually live in small bands of ten to twenty-five animals. If you were to suddenly appear within their view, one goat, usually the watch goat or guardian, would notice you first. He would pick his head up and simultaneously make a gurgling noise in his throat, alerting all the others to look in the direction he was looking. In time, some goats would slowly walk toward you. These would be young males, who are always the most curious. We call it curiosity, but actually these goats are functionaries in a very ordered society who are testing an uncertain and potentially threatening intruder in their home range. Young bucks are the most expendable members of the society and the fastest runners in case things deteriorate. (Our military is well aware of the analogous segment of our society and of its place in the order of nature.) The young males would come closer, stop, move again, expose themselves to danger, even act playful, attempting to get you to make a move—to identify you. If you would suddenly yell and scream and run at them, flailing your arms, all the members of the band would simultaneously contract their hind leg muscles in a split-second crouch-and-bound. What would happen in the next one to two seconds would tell you who's who in the world of caprids.

The young males would run at high speed directly toward the group of females and kids (called fawns in some wild goat-antelopes), who would already be traveling at full tilt toward either escape cover (for instance, steep or rocky terrain or a high point) or just running away (in the case of the North American pronghorn). No special female would be in the lead during this flight, and in fact the "leader" might be a kid out ahead of the group. No order would be necessary. The goats would simply be moving as a tight group. The yearlings and two-year-old males would also be closely packed, following behind the females. (A tight group is not easy for a predator to attack.) If the group contained a weak or lame individual, it would begin falling behind at this time, because the group would be running at the maximum rate for a healthy member of the species.

Meanwhile, most of the older males would be running more slowly behind the younger ones, tracking those ahead from a distance. The remaining old males (usually one, but sometimes two) would have crouched and bounded with all the others, but might only have moved 2 feet, or perhaps 5 or 10 yards. He would then turn around and face the threat. This would be the dominant male. He would be the most aggressive, usually the heaviest, and probably would have the largest set of horns in the group and, having fought many pecking-order battles, would know how to use them. He would place himself between the rest of the band and the threat, leaving no doubt in the mind of any would-be predator that this fellow's job description reads THE PROTECTOR! His position would be in the rear, from whence predators are most likely to attack.

The other adult males would eventually stop and observe the dominant male, ready to back him up in the event of contact with the threat. In the running goat-antelopes, this takes place on the run, with the males breaking into a run to catch up with the herd, the dominant male always last. In the true goats, which are more adapted to jumping and climbing, the tactic covers less ground, with all members of the herd periodically stopping and looking around to assess the circumstances. This truly caprine behavior pattern is a bit more risky to the males. So nature has selected for adult males that often weigh twice as much as females and whose horns are twice as large.

Basically, the male goat's method of defense is to place himself between the predator and the does and kids. True goats will sometimes walk slowly toward a threat, brandishing their horns, and, if the predator doesn't leave, attacking, using the tip of the horns to disembowel. You might think that sooner or later this "Mexican standoff" style of herd defense would result in the decimation of all the older males who, after all, are edible also and very vulnerable, being alone and separated from the group. Well, it's no accident that male goats have scent glands at the base of the horns that secrete various forms of caproic acid. These secretions have a foul, permeating odor and drip down along the neck, where many male caprids have an abundance of hair to hold it, and then down the front legs where it can be seen discoloring the hair. The more dominant the male, the more odor. Also, the more he is dominant, the more a male will practice the unusual habit of urinating on his front legs and neck. The mixture of urine and caproic-acid-related compounds creates an odor that takes male goats right off the menu of any self-respecting coyote or wolf: At least, it seems to confuse the would-be predator. People, of course, are equally repulsed by this odor, and this is one reason we never pack with a buck that is not castrated. (Once a male is castrated, the odor-causing caproic acid, the urine-spraying habit, and the ultraaggressive behavior disappear completely, although the male instinct to protect remains, under the surface.)

It's interesting that the goat-antelopes that can effectively run from predators do not develop any of these traits: They are traits associated with rough terrain. We also see a difference between true goats and goat-antelopes in the daily and seasonal movements of the band. Caprids are generally together as a close unit only on their winter range. If it is time to go to a seep to get a drink (usually once a day on the kidding ground, and so regularly you can set your watch by it), the whole group will string out, often in more-or-less single file, with one female in the lead. This is the "lead female," and the lead goat of the band since the males will usually be behind the females. She also leads migrations to other seasonal ranges and occasionally to new ranges in the event of fire or avalanche destroying a traditional home range, although it is usually the old males that seek out new ranges after a cataclysm. She is always the dominant female in horn-butting conflicts with other females and is usually the oldest breeding female. Pecking-order conflicts occur sporadically all year long in both males and females, especially at times of high irritability in the group (oestrus, rut, prior to storms or earthquakes, and so on).

On kidding grounds and possibly summer ranges, males and females often separate into two groups. This again is a result of the limitations of habitat. Since the safest place for a vulnerable kid is in the most rugged terrain available (cliff ledges usually, or sometimes steep boulder fields where predators feel insecure), and these places are notoriously sparse in food and/or water, the males go off to green pastures, taking the pressure off the limited resources, while the females stay in the safety zone with their offspring. Should a threat occur under these circumstances, the dominant female takes over the role of the dominant male. (Since the female's horns as well as her body size are much smaller than the male's, it clearly is the hostile terrain, not intimidation, that is the primary protector of the band under such circumstances.)

A monosyllabic voice command puts another female "babysitter" in charge of all the young. For some unknown reason, all the little ones will leave their respective dams at this sound and stay with the appointed female. This is done on a daily basis, when the adults go out to feed. The adults take turns at being the babysitter. However, it is always the same female that assumes the position of watch goat or guardian. She is as wary and watchful as her male counterpart in the complete band and may share with him the task of guardian when males and females are together.

Another key position in wild bands of caprids, held by either males or females, is the "social director." His or her job is not to assign things for the group to do, but to make sure that, whatever the group is doing, all members are present and accounted for. If, during a migration, the group goes over a hill and one member doesn't appear in a reasonable amount of time, the social director will stop and make a muted vocalization from the upper throat that stops the entire group until the straggler catches up. He or she is forever looking over the band, apparently counting heads. When this animal dies, another member of the band will step in and fill the position. Physically, the position is in the middle of the group. In fact, if any of the above "job descriptions" is vacated for any reason, it will be quickly filled by another animal who is next in line and who has already been determined by the mysterious group order.

The understanding we need to grasp here is that, in small, tight-unit, vulnerable societies like wild goats, we have a separate but integrated

instinct of the group that works alongside the instincts of the individual and that can, in fact, override the instincts of the individual. When packing domestic goats in the wild, these dormant instincts begin to surface in noticeable ways. The smells, sounds, and appearance of unfamiliar and changing natural scenery trigger an ancient order—migration.

If you are packing more than one goat, you need to think about this. The configuration of your pack string can be critical. If you are packing two goats, you are pretty safe. One switch should take care of a mistake in position, although in one case it wouldn't—if you have two wethers. One is your old, faithful hiking buddy, a ten-year-old, let's say; the other is a brand-new yearling on his first trip. You'd expect the yearling to have a position in front (and so does he), with the older wether in the rear as protector. This would be correct except for one thing. It's perfectly normal for goats to get attached to humans and follow them around. That's why goats were the first domesticated pasture animal. The more they do it, the more it becomes habit. Your old pack goat is used to being right behind you. So, you hike along with two goats behind you, each racing to get ahead of the other until they run right over the top of you. Training and experience will solve this. If you can, just let them tag along until they get tired (a heavy load always helps). They'll work it out themselves. In fact, in most small pack strings, letting the goats work it out for themselves is the best policy. They'll fall into line after a few hours.

With a larger string of five or more goats, you can also let them find their own order, but if your time is important and you're dealing with a group of experienced pack goats, you'll want to help them along.

First and foremost, have a lead goat in the number-one position. If there is an energetic female (with or without a kid), she should be first. If not, the next choice is the youngest, most energetic or friendly wether. No goat wants to be last (since they are all presumably bonded to people, and you're up front), but you must make the best choice. Because this is essentially a migration, the oldest dominant male should be last. For training purposes, a new "trainee" can be put behind the dominant male to learn how to follow in a string. Once he learns, after a few days you can move him up ahead. Don't be surprised if the hind goat puts his head down and gently pushes the wether ahead of him. This is normal and keeps the group moving along. In wild-caprid migrations, the dominant males frequently push underlings with their horns. If there is butting or biting, you must discourage it with a verbal command *No,* or a gentle slap across the nose with two or three fingers. The dominant male is boss and everyone knows it, especially him. If any goats are lagging behind, shorten the lead ropes. A tighter group signals faster walking.

At some point while you're walking free with your goats, you'll probably discover a wether who puts himself in the middle and keeps his head high, watching the others. He's the social director and should be near the middle in a string. The ever-wary watch goat or guardian, who usually seems a bit nervous or high-strung, can be anywhere ahead of the dominant males.

It may take a year or so for a group of goats working and living together to fully accept their roles, and if they get to the wild country only once or twice a year, this order may never fully develop. And it may take you several years as a goat wrangler to get good at spotting who's who in the string. Careful observation will also help you learn your string's strong points and weaknesses.

At water crossings of different widths or boulder fields requiring jumping, goats must be untied to prevent disaster. Even where pack animals must be strung together by law, the law generally says "unless it is unsafe." Safety always comes first.

Well, now you know what to do. Only practice and experience will make your pack string a good one, and you a good goat-packer.

If you happen to run your goats on open range (range allotments), as I do, you can observe in them the social order and band positions we've discussed. It's a fascinating thing to see. The innate programming for group order and division of labor is responsible for the unusual, even neurotic, dependence of solitary goats on their human companions, who, after all, imprinted the little guys as kids to believe that goats and humans are the same species by the simple technique of bottle-feeding.

■5■

Food Along the Trail

PACK GOATS GENERALLY HAVE no trouble finding food. They tend to eat most of the kinds of plants available no matter what area you're in. In the spring, when grass is young and green, they'll eat it. The rest of the year, their preferences shift to more woody plants, including willow leaves and branches (one of the best foods for working goats); low-growing shrubs; pine, fir, and spruce needles; almost any broadleaf-tree leaves and twigs; dead leaf litter and dead bark. Goats also do well on almost all herbaceous forbs, such as dandelions and wild geraniums.

Be careful that your goats don't girdle trees or overgraze one spot. It's the responsibility of the packer, regardless of the type of animal being packed, to manage his stock in a way that limits local environmental damage.

It's a good idea to become at least superficially familiar with poisonous plants in your area through a field guide that discusses toxic plants, or through a local county extension agent. Learn them generally and see if your goat eats them. Goats are very tolerant of a great many poisonous plants that will kill other animals. The ability of goats to denature plant toxins in their gut is legendary, but they still can be poisoned.

As we'll see in Chapter 12, the domestic goat originated as a gene pool from wild animals primarily in the Middle East, Mediterranean, and Central

74

Asian regions—none came from the Americas. Goats do a tremendous amount of "taste testing" from the age of two weeks on—nipping off bits of leaves, flowers, stems, and then moving on to other species. They are feeding the morsels into their genetic computer, scanning the chemical tastes one by one against an ancient analytical program. Most plants have enough chemical similarities worldwide to register correctly as food or poison on the instinctive tastebud sensors. Once identified, plants on the "blacklist" are generally rejected thereafter on the basis of smell. If a plant is not on the blacklist, it will be smelled and eaten quickly in small quantities. If the plant is especially delectable, it will be smelled and gobbled up with impunity. Problems arise when: 1. a plant, not native to the original home range of any of the wild progenitors of an individual pack goat, contains a toxin that the goat is not programmed to detect; and 2. this plant also tastes good. If it tastes good but not extraspecial, the goat will nibble it and move on to the next plant, as goats are prone to do. But if it holds a special appeal, a feeding frenzy may occur, causing too much toxin to be absorbed at one time.

These latter plants are the most dangerous, as death can come quickly to the goat ingesting them. The two most notable in this category are: 1. the very common laurels found east of the Mississippi, in Quebec, and in the Pacific Northwest from northern California to British Columbia (the alpine laurel of the tundra region of the Rocky Mountains does not have this effect); and 2. the wild cherry (principally chokecherry). The cherries are a little different in that the toxic cyanide sugar in the plant is neutralized by an enzyme in the goat called thiocyanate transulferase to become relatively nontoxic and apparently yielding beneficial compounds in the blood. This is good, because goats love to eat large quantities of chokecherry leaves. They taste good. The problem is that if the amount of cyanide sugar ingested at one time exceeds the amount of enzyme in the goat (the toxic threshold), then any additional leaves will be very poisonous. Through most of the year the toxic threshold isn't reached because the bulk of leaves or twigs needed to surpass it is simply too great. But in the springtime, when the leaves are first coming out, or in the fall after drought conditions, the toxic levels in the leaves are greatly increased—and your goat doesn't know this. He can eat the same quantity he did in the summer and be dead in hours from cyanide/benzaldehyde poisoning. A chokecherry tree or bush that is highly toxic usually shows a fair amount of reddish color in the leaves. Symptoms of cyanide poisoning include a bluish color on the inside of the lip or normally pink areas in the mouth, or in the whites of the eyes. Ornamental oleander and castor bean plants are also very toxic, but are not as tasty to goats.

Both laurels and wild cherries are a significant cause of death in goats in North America, not so much on pack trips where people can watch their animals, but under pasture conditions or when goats are used for "weed control." So if you're hiking along and you decide to take a break, don't tie your goat to a chokecherry tree! If left there long enough with nothing else to eat, he may overdo it on the leaves, even in the safe season.

If there is a healthy variety of plants in a backcountry area, it will be unlikely that your goat will poison himself on plants, because goats normally prefer to eat small amounts of a great variety of different plants at any one time, and the toxic ones are thus diluted by the others.

The safest method is to take a little time to check on the poisonous plants in a given area and to keep an eye on what your goat eats. Always let him sample things; that way, he'll learn most of what's good and what's not, but discourage him from pigging out on any questionable plant. Free nibbling and sampling is like a vaccination. It's a little dose of something now that prevents a toxic dose of it later on.

If you're packing a doe, don't forget that some plant toxins are passed on to her milk. Whoever drinks that milk can be poisoned.

Those of us in the Rockies have it easy. We can go anywhere and not be very concerned about toxic plants. Most of what is listed as toxic in plant books here are denatured by goats, and many of the others are simply avoided. I've had to pull my goats away from chokecherries only a few times. You'll have to learn your own area for yourself. Chances are it too will be safe, but it doesn't hurt to ask a local goat breeder for some tips.

The time for your goat to eat is at camp or on short breaks. If you take a water or rest break, let him feed. If you're near a trail, keep your goat at least 6 feet off it so he doesn't damage trailside plants. He will try to nibble en route, especially at the beginning of the day. If this slows you down, or if it just bothers you, you can train him not to do this with a lead rope and a command. Just jerk on the rope as he goes for a plant and say "No!" It'll take a while if this wasn't done during kidhood. Eating is a very strong instinct in goats. He needs to realize that eating itself is fine, but that eating at the wrong time isn't.

In twenty-some years of studying wildlife habitat, I have observed animals of different species graze, browse, and wander in their ranges. I have applied these same techniques of observation to watching my goats in the wild. When in bighorn sheep country, the goats will eat exactly the same plants as the bighorns do, at the same time of year. They will balance their intake of protein, starch, and fats just as accurately as they will go to water at a certain time and drink the right amount. This is the great mystery of instinct—all we know is that it works. Goats have a reputation for eating anything, which is not completely true, but they do have the greatest diversity in their preferred food habits, and this is often mistakenly interpreted as indiscriminate feeding. Nothing could be further

Photograph courtesy of Steve Douglas

from the truth. Watch your goats in the wild for a few weeks and write down what they eat. There will be many plants on the list, but you'll see a very selective pattern of how much of each plant type is eaten each day.

Both wild animals and domestic goats living in the wild also select plants with specific medicinal effects. The literature on this aspect of wild food habits is very sparse. There are specific plants heavily selected for by bighorn sheep, mountain goats, and domestic goats in the wild that are eaten by each species for the "treatment" of specific ailments. This concept is hard for some folks to swallow, but it is built into the biocomputer and is not a whole lot different from the fact that these animals know how to drink more water on a hot day to "treat" dehydration. It happens!

It is no accident that these plants are listed in our books on herbal medicines for treating comparable conditions in humans. This raises the question: Did our knowledge of plant-derived medicines originate with trial and error, or was trial and error the step used in testing easily observed occurrences in nature (i.e., animals eating plants). And if it was the latter method, wouldn't it make sense to observe the animal that can make use of the greatest variety of plant species? Many Native American tribesmen said they learned how to use plants from their teacher the grizzly bear (another animal of very diverse plant utilization). Their ancient knowledge of plant medicines still surprises us today in its effectiveness, and it has added a great deal to modern medicine. The basis of modern medicine, in fact, traces back to ancient Arabic physicians, whose writings are some of the earliest known on any subject in the world, and which were compiled from all over the Middle East, where there were very few bears at the time. But there was the ubiquitous goat, easily observed from the tent door or cave entrance—the only animal with a diet equaling the grizzly's in diversity. Could it be that the goat, revered as a god in many ancient cultures, was the easily observed source of early medical knowledge? I think it's very likely.

But I digress.

This is a good time to address the question of "stones." The goat literature warns owners of male goats to beware of feeding grain or alfalfa to males, and with good reason. After about the age of five, a buck or wether is finished growing. His needs for protein and phosphorus from grain and calcium from alfalfa are greatly reduced. There is a tendency to believe that the goat is somehow unusual among ruminants in that he has difficulty processing calcium and phosphorus after the age of three to five years and will often develop urinary bladder stones. These calculi, or calcium crystals, will grow in the bladder and later break loose and travel out of the body. But because the wether or buck has a constriction at the penis, some stones end up being caught, blocking the flow of urine. This is very painful, and

Photograph by Frandee Johnson

without expensive surgery can end in agonizing death. Productive milking does, of course, do not suffer from stones because calcium and phosphorus are being used in the milk, and any excess can escape daily by way of the udder. In addition, the doe does not have a urinary constriction to block the flow of crystals that may happen to form.

My opinion is that this phenomenon is not a defect in the goat as a species, but rather results from a deficiency of exercise combined with a tendency on the part of goat owners to overfeed grain and other high-phosphorus supplements to increase growth rates. Rule of thumb: If a goat's hooves have to be trimmed, he is deficient in exercise and susceptible to bladder stones. That is, if his hooves must be trimmed, he is either not jumping and running enough on rocks, or his pasture is soft and flat without good goat habitat; therefore, the inspiration for exercise is not there. The end result—a barn potato! The goat in the wild is a very active animal, bounding over rocks and traveling daily from water hole to feeding area until old age (twelve to fifteen years, and occasionally over twenty).

We see in other mammals, including man, the link between exercise and proper calcium metabolism, as in the studies done on muscle use and bone density. Osteoporosis now shows a close relationship to lack of exercise. Maintenance of healthy calcium pathways requires normal exercise. This is as true for domestic goats as it is for domestic humans.

I believe that a goat that works steadily is as healthy as a wild goat if its habitat is goat habitat. It's well known that, although goats do get sick occasionally, they are the domestic herbivore most resistant to disease, and working goats tend to be virtually disease-free. Pack goats, to my knowledge, have never gotten stones if they're used regularly and, generally speaking, they are exceptionally healthy compared to other animals, even dairy goats. Not only do pack goats look healthy as a rule, they also begin to look wild. "Regal" is a term not often applied to goats, but it's one I hear often on the trail from people reacting to seeing a working goat for the first time. Large bones; big chest; smooth, dense coat; perfectly worn hooves; strong pasterns; well-proportioned belly; straight topline; well-muscled body; a look of alertness; a look of intelligence; and handsome horns—these are the marks of a well-bred working pack goat.

■6■

Hooves and Dewclaws

THE GENUS *CAPRA* (WHICH INCLUDES bezoar, ibex, tur, markhor, and domestic goats) and its close relatives are universally accepted as the most agile and surefooted large mammals on earth. For this reason, the subject of traction deserves some special attention. In physics, traction is expressed as the "coefficient of sliding friction." Who cares? you say. Well, your goat cares—and you care for your goat. Just like the butyl polymer tires you have on your car, which stretch and give to conform, on a microscopic level, with the irregular surface of the road, goats have organic polymers in their feet that give and stretch also. The more they conform to those minor irregularities of the ground, the more surface area there is on the hoof and the better its traction. The polymers involved in both cases are long interwoven chains of molecules whose chemical bonds holding the chain together are exceptionally strong. But these chains are only one molecule thick, so that when the mass of polymers rub against the abrasive and immovable surface of rock or pavement, small molecular-sized chunks break off along the entire contact surface, causing wear. If the friction surface didn't wear, it would be too hard to provide good traction (like hard steel) against a road surface.

The most challenging test of traction in rubber tires occurs on racing motorcycles, where a very small surface of rubber must generate enough friction against a road surface to control the high-speed momentum of a 500-pound precariously balanced machine. Racing-motorcycle drivers are meticulously careful about selecting high-traction tires (these are not 30,000-mile tires!). In fact, the best racing tires wear out faster than any other tires and are notoriously short-lived. It's no surprise then, that goat hooves wear down faster than any other hooves.

But hooves, like your fingernails (which, by the way, are made of a very similar molecular polymer), are constantly growing. It follows, then, that caprine animals have the fastest-growing hooves on earth. This is why goat hooves that do not come into contact with their natural medium (rock) must be trimmed every month or so. It also explains why goats don't have to be shod. Horses have to wear horseshoes when worked not because their hooves are soft (goat hooves are actually softer), but because their hoof growth is slower, horses being native to the soft soils of the grassy valley floors of the Middle East. Having to wear iron shoes in the mountains, of course, adds another negative factor to a horse's coefficient of sliding friction. Goats, on the other hand, replace worn hooves so quickly that protection is never necessary. Goat hooves will actually toughen as wear increases, so that the rate of growth is never exceeded by the rate of wear—good news for the goat-packer!

Sore hooves, due to wear, can be the result only of overworking an animal whose hooves have not been prepared by use (a tenderfoot), or may be due to weak or structurally deformed hooves.

If you own your own pack goat, it is your obligation to keep his feet in good shape with periodic exercise. Not only will the hooves toughen and stay trim, but some structural deformities such as splayed toes or spongy pasterns (often genetic tendencies) can sometimes be kept from manifesting with regular exercise. A dry, rocky pen also helps. If a genetic deformity does show up in a way that alters your goat's normal walking, he should not be packed.

An aspect of split-hooved anatomy usually considered vestigial, or useless, is the dewclaw. These look like two knobby, hairless growths lying above and behind the pasterns (and are the toes above the hooves). In large ungulates such as moose, elk, and caribou, dewclaws are enlarged and help keep these heavy animals from sinking in mud and snow. In running caprids, they may be small and nonfunctional or even completely missing, as in the pronghorn antelope. But in the caprine group (true goats), they are especially well developed and extremely functional. For some of the terrain particularly preferred by wild goats, and well suited to goat-packing, dewclaws are absolutely necessary. Where the options for travel are near-vertical rock walls, upward movement is accomplished by the goat's strong, S-curved hind legs, which act like springs. This is why a

pack goat must have a good curvature to the hind legs, as opposed to "posty" (straight-up-and-down) hind legs. Cow-hocked or "hocky" hind legs provide lateral stability and the ability to jump side-to-side, as in bounding up chutes and chimneys.

But coming *down* the same type of terrain is much more difficult, and muscles are not nearly as important here as is traction. *The hind legs are curved so as to engage the dewclaws at just the right angle to provide needed traction for steep declines.* The hind dewclaws always touch down before the front, just as the rear wheel brakes of a motocross motorcycle are always applied before the front ones going downhill to prevent upsetting the center of gravity and flipping the driver over headfirst. The additional surface area of the dewclaws is about 50 percent of the hooves, but the tissue itself is softer and more tractable, so that the actual traction gained is close to 100 percent, thus doubling the original traction.

The goat will actually seek little depressions called "toe holds" in rock to plant his dewclaws in on very steep descents. To do this, a caprid has a very accurate system of visually assessing the minute features of the ground 3-1/2 feet ahead of his eyes as he walks or bounds. He knows exactly where his hind, as well as his front, hooves will be when they get there. A goat's ability to place his hooves in exactly the right place when bounding is nothing short of acrobatic. This detailed eye-hoof co-ordination is learned and developed in kidhood and is why group playtime and proper habitat are important in early training of pack goats. They can learn it later on, but it comes much more naturally to those who played King of the Mountain as kids. Studies of wild caprids have shown a significantly reduced agility and survival rate among adults who grow up alone as opposed to those who could play with other youngsters their own age in those critical six months before sexual maturity.

The goat's peculiar sense of balance allows him, on occasion, to stand on his hind legs, often using his dewclaws for additional support, to eat foliage at the 5- to 8-foot level in trees. He may or may not use his front feet on low limbs. On rare occasions, goats even bound *into* trees, landing on sturdy limbs, and walk around high above the ground feeding on vegetation not available to more grounded life forms. Don't worry, they won't try this with a load on!

■7■
Capricorn

CAPRI: **GOAT/***CORN:* **HORN. CAPRICORN** doesn't mean "goat"! It means "goat horn." The goat horn is probably the most outstandingly unique feature of the goat physique. In caprine species, races, local gene pools, age, heat tolerance, certain personality types, hoof resilience, nutritional history, and breeds can be determined by the horns alone. Horns represent different things to different people: self-defense, threat, majesty. To goats, they are a functional part of the body, serving social, physical, and physiological needs of many descriptions, and I suppose we can say that they have advantages and disadvantages as far as goat owners are concerned.

It is not acceptable in the United States for dairy show goats to have horns. Almost all dairy breeders in this country *disbud* (remove the horn buds with heat or caustic chemical application) both doelings and bucklings (female and male kids) shortly after birth, preventing any future horn growth. Preventing horn growth is considered safer for milk goats, whose pendulous udders are vulnerable, and for goat handlers. It is acceptable for nondairy goats such as Pygmy goats (used as pets) and Angora or Cashmere goats (used for hair production—mohair or cashmere) to have horns. The problem of bodily injury is not so much one of horns as it is of crowding. When confined, goats tend to become more aggressive, and aggressiveness is often expressed by "horning" (even if the horns aren't there). Ironically, one way to reduce aggressive behavior is to leave the horns on, because this aggressiveness is simply a reaffirmation of pecking-order dominance and, once established, is usually carried out visually by brandishing the horns in front of the opponent without as much actual contact. Disbudded adults in dairies sometimes have ugly blisters, scars, or open wounds on the knobs of the head from frustrated, inconclusive pecking-order disputes. Goats without horns are never completely certain who's who in the pecking order, except for Number One—the dominant goat who's usually been around longer than anyone else. This frustration leads to more head-butting.

A frustrated goat, or a goat unbonded with humans, or any breeding male during the breeding season can be dangerous to small children. The presence of horns only increases the possibility of injury in the event of an attack, and an accident can happen with any goat.

I have never found a good reason to remove the horns from any of my goats. At any given time I have some goats that are confined and some that roam free. Milkers live with the wethers, although my breeding bucks are kept separate, and even with fifty to sixty animals in one band, I have never had an injury. But a disbudded goat among his corniferous cousins is a risk, primarily from his frustrated aggressions perpetrated on the smaller animals.

Those are the disadvantages of horns. Let's weigh them against the advantages.

I've already mentioned the use of horn-butting for establishing social order. Once the social order is established, horn displays usually maintain the order with occasional run-ins for recreational purposes (analogous to a bunch of guys shouting and carrying on over a football game at the local pub), and no one gets hurt.

Horns are also weapons used for self-defense. The horns themselves are very sturdy, made of organic polymers (containing keratin) similar to those of the hooves, but harder and thicker so they are not nearly as brittle as bone material (which antlers are made of). Within the hollow horn sheath is a heavy, quickly tapering bone core extending from a thick, porous part of the skull. This has a shock-absorbing effect.

Self-defense is accomplished in several ways. First, the horns are brandished in front of potential threats, such as coyotes, dogs, and other predators. This discourages most predators before any contact is made. If contact is imminent, goats will try to discourage predators by butting—tucking the chin under and aiming the curvature of both horns squarely and accurately at a vulnerable part of the animal. Both the hind legs and the neck muscles are used simultaneously to thrust the horns forward with great force if need be.

If this does not discourage the attacker, a goat will fight to the death. In this case butting is no longer used. Instead, the predator is lured in close by a bluff maneuver in which the goat (usually a male) will stand still, looking straight ahead, perhaps not even looking at the predator, with eyes half-closed (the poker face), and wait until his attacker lunges. Then, with a lightning-quick sideswipe, the tip of one horn is accurately placed in the belly. A quick jerk of the powerful neck muscles raises the point of the horn almost straight up, either opening up the belly or flinging the animal some distance over the goat's back. It is a very effective technique and one reason goats are often used to protect sheep herds. Goats, unlike sheep, will often stand and face a predator, which confuses the predator. A coyote or a dog needs to have its prey run from it to be an effective killer.

Goats have eyesight seven times more powerful than a human's. They are very alert and often stare at threats approaching from a long way off. Once they find out their stealthy approach is being watched, predators seem to be unnerved; they act almost embarrassed and frequently leave, looking back over their shoulders. Because goats cannot outrun predators, they have to outsmart them.

Brandishing horns is akin to a mutually assured destruction policy that keeps the fighting to a minimum. (Not having horns is like having the policy but with the knowledge that there are no warheads in anybody's missiles.) But there are more subtle ways of utilizing weapons—for instance, to show trust. Let me give you some examples.

If two hunters meet in the woods and one aims his rifle at the other, a definite nonverbal statement of aggression is made. This is the same as goats brandishing horns with all the accompanying posturing. If the rifle is held at the hip, pointed in the general direction of the other man, this is equivalent to a goat looking out the side of his head, chin tucked in, leaning his horns sideways at another animal. It is much less threatening if he exposes his side (unless it's a breeding buck during the breeding season, in which case he's saying, "Come on—make my day!"). If the hunter holds the rifle at his side in one hand pointed at the ground, he is saying, "I don't feel threatened." Similarly, the goat will stand at an oblique angle to the other animal in a relaxed posture and not stare at his eyes. Prolonged eye contact is threatening to most animals.

Now let's say the man walks over and leans his rifle against a tree and smiles. The goat will extend his nose slightly (putting his horns back) and stand alongside the other animal, looking at the ground or some nearby object. The goat may even put his nose close to, or against, the other animal's nose in a slow gesture. The man will offer to shake hands. They are both saying, "I trust you." If the goat slowly rests the side of his face and horns on the other goat's face or neck, tilting his head to the side, he's saying, "Hey, Jake! How's my old buddy?" This is total trust and recognition—friendship. A goat will exhibit these same gestures with people. However, a goat not raised around people will tend to use only threatening or neutral gestures.

Gesturing occurs even without horns, but intentions can then be confused. Communications are much more plain and expressive with horns.

Horns also play a physiological role of importance to the goat-packer. All pack animals have their own pros and cons. The goat's major disadvantage is its tendency to overheat. To what degree varies from breed to breed and among individuals. Caprids have several mechanisms for dealing with drought and heat, which we'll discuss in Chapter 8. In addition, goats use their horns to keep cool by circulating large quantities of blood in the porous bone tissue in the lower half of the horn, near the horn sheath. The horn acts as a heat-sink, dissipating the heat by conduction to the air. On warm days, goats will seek out high breezy places where their horns cool even more quickly, and sometimes they will push their horns into damp soil to cool down.*

You can test this yourself. On a hot day, place the palm of your hand on the horn base, close to the head. The temperature will be hot, warmer than any other part of the body—definitely a heat radiator. Since heat regulation will affect the performance of your little friend and let him feel more comfortable, it's a good idea to let him keep his horns, especially if you plan to work him in the desert.

Most caprids butt horns in noisy displays during the rut, or breeding season. Studies of bighorn sheep, a caprid with many similarities to the true wild goats, have shown a definite stimulus and timing effect of horn-butting on the production of reproductive hormones involved in oestrus. Traces of some of these hormones begin showing up in the blood of females thirty seconds after the sound of the clashing horns of nearby rams. These hormones directly affect the receptivity of seemingly unconcerned ewes on the breeding grounds. It's reasonable to suspect that a similar relationship may occur in domestic goats, although the research is yet to be done.

Goats will pack with or without horns. If you feel safer using disbudded ones around your young children, or if you already have keyhole feeders (a slot-type manger that horned goats can't get their heads through), you may opt for hornless goats. Whatever your reason, the decision is yours. You can have a fine pack animal either way.

―――――

*Experiments have shown that when a goat is at rest, three to four percent of its body heat radiates from the horns. When the body heat is raised by exercise, however, heat loss through the horns goes up to twelve percent—a significant increase.

∎8∎

When the Heat's On:
Desert Goats

DOMESTIC GOATS ARE DESCENDANTS OF wild caprids that came from rugged and rocky mountains that were also arid or semiarid—not necessarily hot, because these mountains were higher in elevation than the surrounding country, but dry because most of them were desert mountains, or at least mountains bordering the deserts, of the Middle East and Near East. The drought-tolerant caprids filled this niche, while the camel occupied a similar niche in the more gentle terrain of the lower elevations. Both the caprids and the camelids developed ways of dealing with desert habitats and, more specifically, ways of dealing with scarcity of water. Both store water in their bodies. Where the camel stores water in the fatty tissue of the hump, caprids store it in the blood by increasing the blood volume by about five percent, that is, by diluting the blood with water. This phenomenon was first discovered in the desert bighorn sheep of North America. The camel can amble along for weeks without a drink, and no other animal comes close to that. The domestic goat, under desert conditions, can work three to four days without water. On the other hand, equids—horses and their kin—must have water every day. Their way of dealing with arid climates is to live right next to permanent water holes.

Horses belong to a group of animals called perissodactyls (odd-toed ungulates), who use the last part of their digestive system, the cecum, to digest their food. The food is moved through, quick and dirty, with no attention to detail. Digestion is very inefficient, and both food and water are required in large amounts daily. Horses are adapted to a lush environment where an endless supply of low-quality high-cellulose food (grass) is present, along with water on a daily basis.

Goats, at the other extreme, evolutionarily didn't have it that good. They can take up to four days to digest their food by eating-processing-regurgitating-reprocessing-regurgitating-reprocessing until an efficient breakdown of the nutrients is accomplished. They utilize a wide variety of food types: high and low quality, tender and woody, sometimes even including animal protein. Especially under working or desert conditions, goats have the edge on horses by also being able to recycle urea to help feed microbes in their gut that they later digest as food. This process conserves water because water is not needed to rid the body of urea. It also lowers the goat's impact on its sparse environment by enhancing digestive efficiency. The walia ibex, a rare endemic wild goat of the Simen mountains of Ethiopia, is said never to take a drink, despite an abundance of cool mountain streams in its native habitat. Instead, it seems to obtain all the water it needs from the plants in its diet.

I'm pretty sure that goats' occasional craving for animal protein is somehow related to this urea-recycling process. I've seen it only on long, hot desert trips. The goats will stumble onto an active ant mound and a feeding frenzy begins, with all the goats pushing their noses in to lap up the swarming ants. You'd swear there was a bucket of oats down there, but the frenzy is actually more intense than that caused by grain. They'll lap up all the ants in sight and then paw at the mound, exposing more ants, until there's a large hole in the ground. They may hit one or possibly two more mounds shortly after that in the same manner. This seems to satisfy some inner physiological craving, for they'll then completely ignore ant mounds for a week or even two. But after that, stand back! It'll happen all over again. These ants, by the way, are fairly large red ants that have a nasty bite by human standards.

Goats undergo a transformation when they're working in the desert, which I call their "desert mode." It's like shifting gears—almost like becoming a different species. For example, it's not uncommon for a wether to wait three days to urinate or to wait equally long between free-choice drinks.

By now it must be obvious that the goat is the animal of choice for packing in the desert, unless you happen to have a camel tied up in the garage. (By the way, the llama is a South American camelid, but according to llama breeders, their animals seem to be able to go only two days without

water.) And even if you had a camel, you'd probably prefer a pack goat in the American deserts because many of the most interesting places in our deserts are in the desert ranges, escarpments, lava flows, or rocky desert floors—places often too rocky for the soft-footed camel, but well suited to the goat's hoof. (The camel was put to the test in the Arizona desert by the U.S. Cavalry in the nineteenth century. The experiment ended in the cavalry's rejecting the camel for desert use, in part because the experimental camels' soft hooves were prone to constant injury on the rocky surfaces of the American desert.) A large goat can carry all the water both of you will need for a week.

While all goats use the same methods to prevent dehydration and overheating, some are a little better at it than others. We've already seen many of the desert adaptations of goats, but we need to bring it all together into practical, usable knowledge. Let's spend a few minutes delving into the special attributes of goats in the desert.

Like camels, goats have a widely fluctuating normal body temperature (101.5° to 104.5° Fahrenheit). It moves up and down with the outside conditions of ambient heat and insolation (radiant heat from the sun). People frequently say that goats don't sweat, but actually they postpone sweating by functioning normally at these elevated body temperatures, thus conserving water. This physiological adaptation is technically known as "extending the range of thermoneutrality."

Above a body temperature of 104°, a goat will perspire to promote cooling by evaporation. But just before sweating occurs, he starts breathing through his mouth, instead of his nose, to move more air through the lungs. This cools the body temperature without requiring the large amounts of water used in sweating. When this becomes heavy panting, the goat should be rested in the shade to avoid the sweating stage. Working a goat while he's panting causes a mild form of anoxia (oxygen depletion of the blood), and if the tongue and lips turn blue, you're giving your goat a headache. Better to give him a break—take off his load, including the saddle and pad.

It is always better to rest your goat under shade in the middle of the day in air temperatures above 110° or when working him hard at lower temperatures. If he does begin perspiring, let him sweat freely unsaddled. This way, he'll regulate his temperature while kicking into his desert mode, namely urea recycling and water storage. During this time, goats will not drink or urinate significantly for two to three days at a time. In addition, the general expenditure of energy decreases slightly—enough to notice that there are fewer pecking-order displays and possibly a slowing of walking speed. Laying the pack cover lengthwise over the neck and pack will help keep him cool, as will wet rags placed in the same way.

I strongly believe in leaving horns on pack goats, especially if they will be working in the desert. The radiation of heat from the horn base (as we learned in Chapter 7) is similar to the cooling fins on an air-cooled engine. Break off those cooling fins and the engine overheats. On those 120-degree days, you can make your goat "water-cooled" by wrapping a wet bandanna loosely around each horn base, wetting them down again when they dry out. (Between the beard, headband, and backpack, your goat will look like a sixties hippie, but he's much less likely to protest!)

I like to carry at least one silk scarf (24 inches square or larger). Silk makes the best horn-cooler and neck-cooler for both man and beast; it's a bug filter for fresh goat milk, an emergency collar for goats, mosquito netting for your hat and face while you're sleeping, shade for the back of the neck (both goat and goat wrangler), an emergency sling or bandage, and has a thousand and one other uses.

You may want to carry a fly for midday shade, but in most deserts your goat will seek out shade under bushes or arroyo walls. Caves are the best. A twenty-minute rest in a 60-degree cave will revitalize you both enough for a few more hours of high desert heat, plus conserve a tremendous amount of water.

I happen to have a fondness for moonlight hiking in the desert. It's another world after dark, and you use much less water. Goats have exceptionally keen night vision and prefer packing when it's not so blisteringly

Photograph by Jeff Corney

hot. In daytime packing, be prepared for the spectacle of pronghorn antelope, wild horses, or desert bighorn sheep moving in on you. They all
tend to be intensely curious about pack goats. Use caution around stal-
lions, however. They can be dangerous at close range.

Goats love basking in the sun in the morning, especially on bitterly
cold days in the midwinter Wyoming mountains. They will stand perfectly
motionless, perpendicular to the solar rays, eyes half-closed, for hours in a
state of catatonic caprinity! A person gazing upon the serene sight of a pristine snow-covered mountainside dotted with dozens of sleepy-eyed caprine
pasture potatoes finds himself lulled into a warm, meditative complacency
unrivaled by any yogi—truly one of the major benefits of goat-keeping.

Of all the American breeds, Saanens seem to be the most fond of
basking in the sun. The Saanen breed produces excellent pack animals
of above-average load capacities due to their size and big-boned structure.
They are very tolerant of cold mountain conditions and do well sleeping
in the snow. They have high energy in winter and make perfect sled goats
in harness. In desert conditions their performance is the poorest. They
can still pack, but their endurance is very much limited by the heat.
Clipping their hair does help, but they are still limited. A good Nubian
can outlast any Saanen in the desert. It goes without saying that any of
the other packable breeds can, as well. I believe this is due to the Saanen

having a genetic makeup partially composed of a subarctic wild goat (probably domesticated in or near Mongolia).

Saanens tend to start panting (like a dog) sooner than do other goats, and this attempt at releasing heat from the body lowers the oxygen intake and, correspondingly, the endurance. They also begin to sweat at lower air temperatures. Sweating as a cooling method uses up precious water, so Saanens have to drink more and can't go as long without drinking. Saanens need to be exposed gradually to intense sunlight if they normally use a barn or have just had their hair clipped, because their low-pigment skin can burn or even get sun blisters. They have a lower tolerance to the sun. All in all, a Saanen is not a happy camper in desert conditions above 90° Fahrenheit.

Let's compare the other breeds under conditions of heat stress.

The Cashmere is essentially the same as the Saanen.

The Toggenburg is, for the most part, a Saanen in Toggenburg clothing. Its horns are exactly the same as the Saanen's in size, shape, and color, indicating a very similar ancestry. None of the other dairy breeds has the large, curving, unpigmented, scimitar-shaped horns with large basal perimeter. Toggenburgs, however, show some additions to their gene pool. They have brown hair with a tan-gray-pigmented skin that eliminates the solar sensitivity problems of the Saanen. They are also, on average, a bit smaller, shorter, and a little more heat-tolerant.

All the other available breeds have black horns that are thinner and shorter with a smaller basal perimeter, black or mottled black/gray/pink skin, and variously colored pelage. As a rule, black-horned goats have greater heat tolerance. If your goat doesn't have horns, black-horned goats also have black hide under the hair (as do most wild desert ungulates).

The smallest horns occur on Nubians, which make up for this shortcoming by having the largest ears. Large pendulous ears with enlarged blood vessels radiate heat in the same manner as do large ibex-type horns, and are common in many species of desert mammals throughout the world. If you have a Nubian that happens to work well, he should be a high-endurance desert animal. The slick, shiny hair that most Nubians have is always better for heat-tolerance than a coat that is scruffy and dull.

Since many pack goats are crossbred, you must judge the animal by dominant visible traits, like horn color and description, skin color, hair type, and the shape of the ears. Nubian crosses with other breeds often have what are known as "airplane ears" that stick out horizontally, neither upright nor pendulous. They are thicker than upright ears and have "ribs" that run lengthwise, as well as enlarged blood vessels. These ears also act as heat radiators. A Saanen/Alpine cross with Saanen coloring will have Saanen physiology and tolerances. In my experience, any crosses of

Alpine, LaMancha, and Oberhasli show the greatest endurance under desert conditions.

Goats use up various salts (especially sodium chloride—table salt) rapidly when working, and even more so under desert conditions. They will crave salt after a few days and will get it from eating plants in the goosefoot family (Chenopodiacae), common in desert flora and especially the northern salt scrub deserts of the West's Great Basin. They will often lick roots and even begin eating clay soils for salt. This is okay. It's the way caprids get their salts in the wild, but since pack goats are working a little harder than they would in the wild, it's better to carry salt for them. A pocket-sized mineral block will do wonders for their metabolism and spirits. Let them lick it once a day, but hold it tightly—they may try to swallow it whole. Never leave it out where they can get at it, because it could make them awfully sick if it were swallowed whole. I like to carry salted pumpkin seeds on pack trips. You can pop the seeds for yourself and feed the shells to the goats. Both the roughage and the salt are good for them, and I haven't met a goat yet that didn't find them irresistible. I also feed my goats some of the whole seeds as a supplemental feed/treat—two handfuls a day per goat is enough.

■9■

Glacier Goats

THIS CHAPTER COVERS HIKING AT THE OTHER END of the spectrum— the barren land at the top of the world, the upper limit of the highest vegetation zone—the glaciers.

The alpine tundra is a harsh high-elevation zone of rock, ice, low temperatures, short summers, wind, the hardiest plants in the world, and the hardiest animals—the caprids. Worldwide, the only group of large land herbivores tough enough for this environment is the caprids (goats and their close relatives). Others migrate in for the heat of the summer, spend a month or two, and then leave for warmer climes. With the exception of the polar bear and the wolf, way up north in many areas caprids are the only large critters who actually prefer this environment year-round. Some examples are: in the East, the Himalayan tahr, Caucasian tur, markhor, blue sheep (not a true sheep but a goat-relative of the tribe Caprini), Japanese serow, Siberian ibex, alpine ibex, Spanish ibex, urial, sheep argali, sheep, and snow sheep; in the Alps, the chamois, also a relative of the mountain goat; in East Africa, the walia ibex; and in North America, the mountain goat (actually a goat-antelope), musk ox (not an ox at all but a goat-antelope of the tribe Ovibonini), and bighorn and thinhorn sheep (goatlike sheep). Caprids occur not only in the arctic and

subarctic, but throughout the Ice Age remnants of the cordillera (the term collectively describing the high mountain chains of western North America). Glaciers are among the most pristine lands still left in North America, and some of the most beautiful, as many hikers are discovering. Much of this intriguing land is also rugged, bordering on inaccessible. A good percentage of it is inaccessible to almost all pack animals. Except the goat—the only pack animal whose ancestry is native to this inhospitable grandeur.

Where the horse trail ends is what we goat-packers call the trailhead. Where the llamas have to turn back, that's where the backcountry begins. Glacier country is too rugged even for a lot of backpackers, unless they can shed some of their load. Goats have to be packed lightly in some of this difficult terrain, but at twenty percent of its body weight, on average a pack goat is still carrying 40 pounds.

Once in the tundra, goats relish the common plants considered unpalatable by most other animals: leathery and woody dwarf specimens of the heath family (Ericaceae), like the purple mountain heather that blankets the ground; alpine willows (about 2 inches tall); sedges; and innumerable tundra wildflowers. They devour large quantities of the bitter-tasting western yarrow, which speeds up their adjustment to high elevations. Climbing higher, this lush skyscape wanes into a rock garden of gray granite and blue sky dotted with white snowfields and white clouds. You can almost see your goats smiling. Something inside says this is home to them. It all of a sudden becomes clear why, back at the pasture, goats normally eat on the run, going from one plant to the next, nipping off little bits of the tops of a great variety of species. Up here it's the only way. All you get is a little nip at a time, then you must go find the next plant, probably a different type: opportunistic feeding.

Goats can go for months without drinking liquid water (sometimes the better part of a year). When all the water's frozen, eating snow comes naturally to a goat. With the exception of does producing milk, pack goats often prefer nice, clean, white snow to questionable water. (By nature, they will take the cleanest water available, but if the cleanest water available is a mud hole, they will suck it up with gusto, just as their wild counterparts would. If they learn this as youngsters from watching adults, there is no aversion to it.) Goats are very dexterous with their front feet, and usually a dozen or so scrapes with a front hoof will clean away any surface debris and expose a pure layer of spotless graupel snow, which goats savor at high elevations.

They will scratch at the ground, even turn over rocks with a hoof, just to see what's underneath. As their calloused knee patches attest, they will often get down on their knees to stretch their necks over a cliff just to sample a green morsel. Their joy at being in the place for which they are so fully adapted shows in their unbridled curiosity. Pushing above 12,000 feet, goats feel more secure. There are few predators at this elevation. Mountain lions are mostly below us now, and the few lone coyotes you see up here don't look happy—desperate may be the best description. They may be ready to take on a hoary marmot or a red-backed vole, but not the great noble beast of the tundra, a horned caprid who's feeling in his element!

Rocky Mountain bighorn sheep come to investigate, and like their distant cousins the domestic sheep, seem to have an irresistible urge to follow goats, even with brightly colored Primates intertwingled. (Historically, goats have been kept with sheep for two reasons: 1. horned goats can protect sheep from predators; and 2. because goats are more easily trained and sheep tend to follow goats, goats can lead sheep out to a certain point to graze during the day and bring them back before dark.)

The bighorns' fear of man is overcome by the attractive forces of kinship. The caprids speak to one another among the peaks for miles, sheep behind the goats. But they speak in tongues unintelligible. The sight of familiar armaments and the smell of caprid esters (chemical identifiers) are lures that eventually end in frustration—a failure to communicate, a capricious Tower of Babel at 12,000 feet. The bighorns retreat back to the interior of their home ranges as the goats step into the clouds and beyond.

High above the clouds, between 13,000 and 14,000 feet, where the mountains actually meet the sky, the air is thin. Rest breaks are more frequent. Time is taken to inhale—not just air, but the sky as well. It's cold and brisk and smells blue, a stark contrast to the only other color, the white that stretches as far as the eye can see and suspends your pack string somewhere between the ground and the sky. *Terra firma* is a thousand feet below, and the goats are still very much in their element on the glacial ice. Testing the glacier for weak spots, staying away from large dark areas that may be insidious granite surrounded by a hollow pocket of air, which will support neither man nor beast, they move on. One behind the other, horns glistening in sunlight so intense that humans will sustain retina damage without glacier goggles (the slitted caprid eye is perfectly adapted for living in the sky), they traverse to the top of the glacier.

In time, we come to islands in the sea of ice and snow. Like islands in the ocean, they are the tips of lofty mountain peaks, some close to 14,000 feet, sticking up through the solid water we walk on. We can even see shoreline at times on one side or the other. These islands and shores are the key to goat-packing in the glacier country, and your animals will instinctively head straight for them if allowed to lead the way.

Glaciers are notorious for quickly changing weather that can be gloriously sunny and warm one minute, only to be followed by a cold ground blizzard with whiteout conditions and fifty-mile-an-hour winds the next. If vision can be used at all, it's to see large dark objects like rock islands between wind gusts. I've experienced glacier ground blizzards so extreme that breathing felt like drowning, with wind blowing snow into the nose and mouth from every direction. (Another use for the silk scarf—placed under your hat and tucked into your jacket, you can see through the silk, even while wearing glacier goggles, and breathe through this effective snow filter. After the storm this same arrangement can protect you from sunburn and snow blindness if you've lost your goggles in the wind and have no other protection.)

Rock outcrops may be the only shelter from the wind and, without supplemental feed, the only source of food for your goats. Above 13,000 feet there doesn't seem to be anything growing in the rock, but as you get up close to the rock surfaces, the dull gray of the granite is bespeckled with brightly colored splotches of orange, green, black, yellow, and red. These are lichens, a union of fungal and algal life forms that break down rock and form flat vegetative masses on the rock face. The fact that these primary digesters of postglacial environmental debris are the only resident life forms, other than a single-celled alga living invisibly in the snow, makes this place the most primitive ecosystem on earth. No large animals can live here year-round, but goats are equipped with teeth in the lower jaw capable of scraping these small vegetables off the rocks. They can, in fact, survive for some time on them, especially if supplemented by a couple of handouts every day of COB (corn, oats, barley) or pelletized alfalfa and grain. In addition, goats like to bed down on these rock outcrops at night. Although they can bed down on glacial snow, bedding on the rocks will be warmer and drier and thus keep their energy up for an extended stay. Goats also love to play on these glacial rubble piles. To a goat, it's an island paradise.

Moving out across the ice, I often rely on my goats for "back-pulling," to add extra stability where slippery conditions prevail. Goats will usually pull back on the lead rope with a steady pressure on a slippery descent. Although you must read conditions to be sure you won't pull your animals off balance, if the human members of a pack string are roped together and one of them should fall on a descent, the sudden jerk on the lead rope will cause the goats to pull back and dig in with a per-goat force exceeding that of a strong man (remember, the goat has four sharp points of traction supporting a 200-and-more-pound animal). However, any time goats are used for back-pulling, the lead rope should be attached to a neck collar instead of a head halter. The neck is in a stronger position for pulling (wethers have extremely strong neck muscles), and using a collar reduces the risk of injury to the goat to almost zero.

Climbing up or descending steep glacial topography is easy for a pack goat. Even loaded, he is more surefooted than a man with crampons (removable spikes that are fastened onto hiking boots for traction on ice).

Packing with goats at high elevations is doubly rewarding because it's pleasing to see an animal working in its native habitat, in the place to which it is most suited. Saanens and Toggenburgs of large stature are probably the best for this kind of travel, although any packable breed will work.

Glacier Tips

1. Exposure at these elevations while working hard, especially during the first day or two, may cause dehydration in both you and your goats. If they look sluggish and/or develop the appearance of a slight ring around the eye (on the hide on the lower eye socket), heat up some snow and take a warm-water break at camp (you can add a little molasses to the water to make the goats drink more). Pass the mineral block around, too.

2. Don't forget that when feeding in bighorn sheep country, goats can pick up lungworm from plants. A regular worming plan should be followed annually.

3. As always, your goats should have veterinary inspections periodically, and be careful to keep your goats healthy and clean. The wildlife veterinarians who have studied the issue to date agree that pack goats are as safe as llamas to use around wildlife, but we absolutely don't want to take any chances of introducing new diseases to the wild—especially to the more susceptible caprids like mountain sheep or mountain goats, or even to pronghorn antelope. It's easy to be careful, and both your animal and the wild ungulates will be better off for it.

Photograph by Jeff Corney

There is a special treat you can take advantage of if you happen to have a milking Toggenburg doe on the glacier. I call it Toggen Daz Glacier Ice Cream. (Actually, any breed of doe will work just as well.) You make it with goat milk stirred into glacial graupel (surface granular snow) with honey and cornstarch for thickener (pudding mixes can be substituted for the honey and cornstarch). Add some wild berries, such as huckleberries, you've collected earlier and brought to the glacier. Make sure you don't use red snow. It is tainted with a toxic form of algae (*Clamaedemonas nivalis*) that can make your eyes photosensitive. In sufficiently large quantities, it can also make you very ill. (Yellow snow can have similar effects, for purely psychosomatic reasons.)

The Toggen Daz is delicious, nutritious, and good for the spirits when served in an old dented tin cup with little red and purple umbrellas sticking out of it. After the kids (yours and the goats') have gone to bed, you can serve the leftovers with a bit of blackberry brandy poured over the top. It makes a great warmer-upper and nightcap!*

---

*Goat milk is an efficient way to convert the national forest into good-tasting, nutritious protein. Although it is much less likely to harbor disease organisms than cow's milk, some people prefer to pasteurize the milk rather than drink it raw. This is done simply by carrying along a thermometer and heating the milk to 165 degrees for five minutes.

▪10▪
Training

THROUGHOUT THIS BOOK I HAVE PASSED ALONG a number of training tips, but if you're interested in acquiring a kid and working with it, there are a few more things you need to know.

First and foremost, make sure you have a reasonably good kid to begin with. You don't want to make an investment in time and feed only to find out a year later that you have a Pygmy, or a lame animal, or a goat that just won't pack. Lovable goats are easy to come by—they're everywhere. Don't be swayed by temperament alone. Check into a goat's history; meet his parents and grandparents if possible. Look at his feet, legs, body length, leg length, height, and coat. You want a healthy animal with bright eyes, shiny coat, a long and tall build, long stride, strong feet, and a good curvature of the hind legs.

Of course, the best way to get someone's goat (so to speak) is to go to someone who knows and raises pack goats. At this writing, such persons are few and far between, but rapidly growing in number. They can sell you a kid, adult wether, doe, or buck and answer your questions. In addition, some dairy-goat breeders have some working-goat-quality animals for sale. Check around. If you know goats, sometimes you can go to the livestock sale barn and come home with a fine little wether for around $40,

Photograph by Steve Alden

or whatever the local goat-meat prices are. However, if you don't know goats, you're more likely to come home with a genetically small, possibly abused or lame animal who'll never pack well. Nevertheless, due to the nature of the animal, the low overhead associated with keeping them, their high reproductive rate, quick-to-learn nature, and friendly attitude toward trainers, goats will always be a less expensive way to go than any other alternative.

After you've chosen an animal, you must begin the training program. The steps are simple. How much time you put into it is up to you.

Bonding

This is critical to all further training and is usually started at birth or shortly thereafter by bottle-feeding or daily one-on-one playing. Bonding is achieved by physical contact and the development of trust. It is something that comes more naturally to goats than to any other species, except maybe dogs and humans.

A bottle-fed kid taken away from his dam at birth will bond quickly to you and want to follow you everywhere. Let him follow you every day for a while. However, the young goat must learn that there is a time for play and affection and a time for work. He needs to learn there are

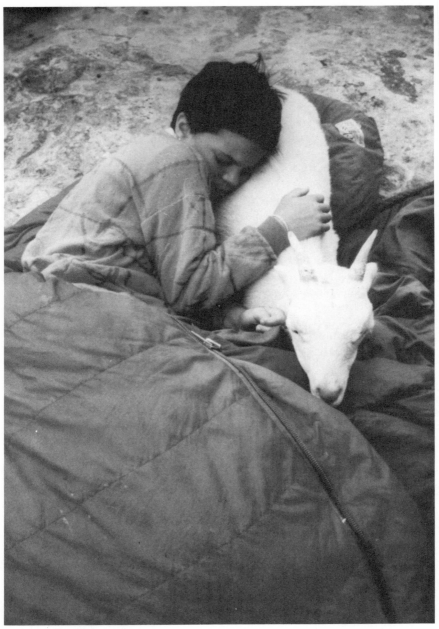

Photograph by Steve Alden

things he can get away with and things he cannot. Do not give in to his crying for your attention or you'll create a noisy goat. Goats, by nature, get lonely without company, so it's always a good idea to have more than one. Three or four kids is ideal. Two will do the trick. Playing, kid-style, will develop skills pack goats need later in life. A pack-goat breeder considers kid groups in good rocky goat habitat a part of the training process. The kid must bond to you as well as to other goats. Occasionally meeting other animal species (horses, dogs, llamas) is also good experience. The word "capricious" means goatlike and whimsical and perfectly describes the behavior of the young goat. His sudden jumps in the air, somersaults, bounding off of fence posts, watching imaginary bugs jumping and flying, running in circles at high speed, then jamming on the brakes, plus myriad facial expressions, are all ways of exploring his environment and becoming part of it. The fact that these things so readily make us smile and want to hold this crazy little fuzzball in our arms reflects the interspecies attractiveness that made the goat the first domesticated herbivore, and also makes a kid likely to become a spoiled brat in the wrong hands. You *must* be consistent. And never let him in the house! His house is his, and your house is yours!

If you give in too often to your kid's whims, eventually you'll have a 250-pound brat who expects to have his own way—and at 250 pounds he's got a good chance of getting it! Yes, goats can throw a tantrum, hold a grudge, and try to "get even" when the time is right. Remember, you're dealing with an intelligent animal. Also remember that your hard-working, well-trained, mature pack animal is approximately a three-year-old by human mental standards.

Punishment is sometimes appropriate but should never be intended to inflict damage, or even much pain—only shame. Two or three fingers lightly slapped across the nose, accompanied by a disapproving tone of voice, is almost always enough.

Most training and behavior modification should come in the form of praise for a job well done. Rewards are essential and may include COB in small handouts, stroking, petting, scratching in the favorite places (such as the jowls), rubbing behind the horns or behind the ears, petting the neck or back, even hugging. Your goat will let you know what he likes best. All the above should be accompanied by verbal encouragement, words of praise, or any enthusiastic displays of a positive nature.

Forcing a goat to work for you does not produce the best results. A goat is an independent "free spirit" who loves company but hates being forced to do anything. You can make the most of that trait. If you will let him work for you because he wants to and urge him to overcome weariness, boredom, or discomfort with words of encouragement and friendship

and rewards that will keep him happy and interested, you will have an animal that seems to be continually asking, "What can I do for you next?" He'll be a delight to be around, and he'll come to think of you the same way. He'll enjoy working for you as much as you enjoy rewarding him, and you will equally enjoy each other's company.

Leading

Teaching a goat to lead is very important for many later skills. Do it right and you'll save yourself lots of trouble later.

First, take your goat away from and out of sight of all other goats. Let him follow you around a little bit and give him a few morsels of grain and some comforting strokes and words. Then attach the lead rope to his collar. Walk around and let him become familiar with it. If he tugs back, let him fight it, but don't give him any slack. When he stops fighting, talk to him gently and offer him some grain in your hand, but make him come and get it. Repeat this again and again, luring him forward with the grain until it starts to become habit to follow the rope.

When you pull on the rope, always use a voice command such as "Come on, boy." Be consistent with your words. When you stop, say "Whoa" at the same time you pull back on the lead rope. Shorten the rope as you make progress to make his responses to the lead more precise. By the way, if you're planning to use him as a harness goat later on, you should also teach him verbal commands for right and left, usually "Gee" and "Haw," respectively. At first, you should limit training sessions to about ten minutes of every thirty to sixty minutes, because kid goats have a short attention span.

Use the word "Easy," said in a calm, comforting way, to get him to stand still. Hold his collar with one hand and stroke him with the other until he stands calmly. Then give him some grain. Repetition will make all these responses patterned behavior.

If you don't have time for these procedures, or if they're not working quickly enough, you can tie your goat to a drag (a log or old tire) that is almost too heavy for him to pull, with about 15 feet of 1/2-inch rope. Do this for a whole day at a time when you can keep an eye on him—you don't want him to get hurt. After two or three days of this he'll learn to respect a rope, and by then he should be ready to lead and be picket-broke.

General Training Tips

Once he leads well, you can go on to more ambitious lessons—like jumping up into a truck, walking logs, crossing streams, crossing logs over streams, swimming, and more verbal commands. All are easily accomplished with a young goat, some trust, and time. A small handful of COB at just the right time will make short work of most training exercises.

A note of caution: As a young wether grows and his horns become more prominent, you may be tempted to restrain him by grabbing a horn. His horns may resemble handles, but they definitely are not! *Never* grab a goat by the horn (unless you're training rodeo goats). It will only cause him to use his horns later on in human relations. The concept of using his horns on a human for any purpose whatsoever would never pop into the head of a properly trained working goat. So don't give him the idea.

Similarly, as an adult on the trail, your doe or wether can still learn bad habits, so you should also discourage bystanders and fellow hikers from grabbing your goats' horns. Some people find this irresistible, but it triggers the goat's defenses in a negative way, just as grabbing a stranger's rifle while he's out hunting in the woods would. If this is done often enough, a goat will begin brandishing his horns or even butting people when they approach too quickly. This should not be allowed to happen! A goat that is allowed to do this can become a dangerous animal, and you may become the target of a lawsuit. As a packer on public land (or anywhere else), you are responsible for your animal's actions and must have control of him. *Never let anyone grab your goats' horns!*

Training a goat to walk in water is not at all difficult if you start early. Goats have a natural fear of water that is very strong, but it doesn't kick in until about three months of age. If he's trained before that time and the training is periodically reinforced by walking him in streams and lakes with you, he'll grow up without a significant fear of water. Of course, if you don't think you'll ever cross water in your journeys, you may not want to spend the time.

With young kids, just let them follow you into irrigation ditches, streams, ponds, and so on. Start shallow and, day by day, get into deeper and deeper water until, after several weeks, the kids are swimming. It's difficult for some goat owners to believe, after seeing how powerful the natural fear of water is, that many adult goats, when trained early, can actually enjoy going into a lake to cool off or to swim.

The key to successful water training is to feed your animal grain while you are both standing in water. Also, stroke him and talk to him. Spend as much time as you can in the water. If physically possible, give him his daily ration of grain every day for two weeks in a stream or lake, and nowhere else. At the end of that time you will have a goat that can be trained to fight his way across rushing rivers or swim behind your canoe on portage trips.

Retraining an older goat whose fear of water is already developed is

Photograph by Steve Alden

a much more challenging task. It may take months, and he may still balk at stream crossings. You might have to pull him in to get his feet wet before he will cross. At that point, you'll be glad he weighs only 200 pounds instead of 800!

When crossing streams in the backcountry, goats will usually investigate all other options to getting their feet wet, even if they are trained. It's my opinion that they have difficulty seeing through the surface of water, so even a shallow stream could be a hundred feet deep as far as they know. Bounding from rock to rock is a popular goat method for crossing a stream, as is walking a log. Jumping is most common if the water is less than 5 feet wide. I have a 250-pound wether who has jumped an 8-foot span several times, fully loaded. Goats are good jumpers, with legs like springs for smooth takeoffs and landings.

Be careful not to let your buddy have a bad experience with water early in his career, or he may remember it every time he has to cross water in the future.

I once tried a tricky rock-stream crossing with a string of seven seasoned packers and a yearling on his second trip. Normally, I'd have untied the string on this crossing, but the Forest Service in one district had a rule that goats and llamas must be strung together at all times, and I wanted to see if this kind of crossing was possible. Well, all went well until the

yearling (number three in line) decided to jump instead of stretching a little and walking across two rocks. This jump pulled the goat behind, who also jumped, but had no place to land on the little rock. Instead, he bumped the yearling and landed in the you-know-what, which pulled the off-balance yearling in backward, as well as the two goats in the lead who were not looking behind and who were unprepared for the backward pull. The three remaining well-trained wethers in the rear responded automatically to the tug on the lead rope by going forward and trying to jump over the writhing caprine biomass in the streambed below, only to hit the end of the lead rope, one by one, and become one with it. It was all horns and hooves for a while, as I struggled to untangle the jumble before someone drowned. This was, by far, my worst wreck ever—2,100 pounds of goats and cargo compressed into one soggy amoeboid amorphism about the size of a Volkswagen.

Once we were out of the drink and assessments were made, there were no bodily injuries, although one stainless steel pot required some serious reshaping, and several bags of bananas and peaches were rendered unfit for human consumption. Somehow the squeezebox emerged unscathed.

Pack goats are tough animals. Admittedly, this was pushing it a little, but working goats almost never get hurt. The experience left its mark, however, which was apparent at the very next stream crossing. These veterans of the wild slowed down long before the water's edge and, even after being untied, looked cautiously at the water, then at one another, then at the water. They eventually crossed with huge distances between them, making absolutely sure they weren't tied together. It was half the summer before they took stream crossings in stride again.

I learned a good lesson: If you think even one goat may jump in questionable terrain, break up the string. A real good pack string can be led through a river with water up to their backs without problems—as long as they don't have to jump while tied together.

Young wethers (and does) can be hooked into a string when they're about six months old. Always put them in the rear of the pack train and let them stay in that position at least a full day. Older goats being trained as work animals for the first time also learn fastest by starting out in the back of a pack string. They will want to catch up with the other goats, so the incentive to keep moving and following the lead rope is there. They're not as likely to question where everyone's going, as with some other species (no matter how faithful to humans they may be). A goat that does not want to learn to lead will learn at the tail end of a pack string. The goat-packer has to watch the string carefully during these training sessions, especially where the trainee can go around the wrong side of a tree or hesitate too long on a switchback and be pulled through the rocks. Serious injuries are possible if you're not watchful. Don't be afraid to give the trainee a heavy cargo at this time; if he is too lightly packed, he may have too much excess energy and want to run ahead. He must learn to stay behind. A narrow trail helps with this, as well. Once the trainee gets a little tired, he will begin to learn. This applies to all pack training. A goat that is feeling tired (just like a person who is learning to hike) is going to discover ways to make packing easier on himself—like following his lead rope, keeping his pack from banging into trees and rocks, staying on the trail (where there is one), and honoring the requests of the trainer. This is why it is so important for you as trainer not to give in to the weaknesses of the animal. Sure, you can give him a break, but right after the break he will have to complete the job given him. Once he realizes he has to do what's asked of him, he'll learn that it's easier to just do it than to fight it. If he's a little tired from carrying a load, he will learn twice as fast. A good trainer will realize the value of a healthy working fatigue without taking it to the point of exhaustion, which would eventually give the goat a negative attitude toward packing.

A goat's gregarious instinct to keep up with the herd can be used to maintain a positive attitude while he is learning. If he feels forced or driven by you, he will have a negative attitude toward people. If, however, he can be made to believe he is spending this energy for himself, trying to keep up with his buddies in the "band," or with you, and if he succeeds in that attempt, he will feel good about himself and the whole experience. Always try to work *with* your goat's instincts rather than against them.

With this in mind, you can accomplish the very important and ongoing task of conditioning by letting your buddy follow you on increasingly longer hikes. The more you exercise him, the stronger his muscles get. One- or two-mile walks on weekends are good and can be made even better with the addition of 30- to 40-pound loads; five miles a day is better still. Do what you can. If a few miles a month is all you can do, it's better than none, but remember that your goat's performance will depend as much on the condition of his muscles as on his training.

When getting a trainee used to the pack saddle, put it on him and give him a little grain. Then let him wear it half a day. Do that several times around home. Then add the panniers and go out and stroke him periodically. Then go for walks with him with his tack on, just the two of you at first, then in a group. If you postpone the direct association of saddle and tack with heavy loads, he will positively associate it with fun outings with the old man (or old lady).

A wether's relationship to you should always be something on the order of child to parent, even long after he has severed his natural filial link with his dam. Wethers can be suspended in that relationship most of their lives with a human if a positive relationship exists. Does and bucks usually begin resisting this after about their second year, although the friendship part of the relationship will remain strong. This resistance will appear as an independent streak, particularly noticeable in Toggenburgs, although they will still pack well. It will start to be apparent in wethers by age four but can be kept in check by knoodling and attention-giving behavior on your part.

Knoodling may actually be the most important aspect of training and maintaining a good pack goat. To knoodle with an animal is to fondle, stroke, massage, and generally display your affection for him. This includes talking to him calmly and playing his favorite tunes on your squeezebox. It boils down to repeated reassurance, which in time becomes expected. Part of the loyalty goats show for humans is dependence on interpersonal contact, which is simply the displaced instinct for intercaprine dependence —what we call the "herd instinct." It is difficult to force a goat to do anything he doesn't want to do, but he can be encouraged to do whatever *you* like in the name of maintaining herd instincts. This is partly why he will follow you anywhere (almost). The other reason? It's the nature of the goat to be tempted to follow humans, just as it's the nature of sheep

Photograph by Frandee Johnson

to want to follow goats. Why? We don't know—maybe because God said it's okay—so why not make the best of it?

Rarely, there will be a young goat that, despite possessing every genetic reason to be a great pack animal, will not follow or respond well to training. He may often seem lethargic, lack energy, and even look sick (although sometimes he will appear healthy). Do not waste your time on him. This kind of personality will never work out. Trade him in on a new one. For the pack-goat breeder, culling is the most important part of turning out reliable animals.

Sometimes a goat will do something that is absolutely inexcusable, and you'll need a special training tool—behavior modification! Inflicting pain is not an effective way to focus a goat's attention. Surprise is! The caprine mentality respects creativity.

One time, a year-and-a-half-old wether named Tin Cup gave me the old broadside "Come on, make my day" look. This was to be expected, because he was cut (castrated) late. (I cut him after he was one year old instead of one month old, which is a good way of using a particularly fine animal for breeding one time before using him to pack.) Late-cut animals are good to have in a herd or a pack string because they will naturally fill the niche of protector, having developed some of the protector patterns of thinking, which they will forever retain. They are especially protective (defensive) around "their" animals, particularly females and kids, but even wethers. They also can become more aggressive around people, especially when crowded.

Well, it was raining, and all the animals were crowded into the shed. I bent over to pet one of the does. Next thing I knew, I was stacked up against the goat-shed wall and old T.C. was trying to look innocent (if he could whistle he'd have been doing it!). But it didn't work. I got up, slowly walked over to him, and latched on to his collar. His eyes got big as moose turds and seemed to say, "Uh oh—I think I shouldn't have done that!" Slowly I led him over to a rafter where I keep an old, stale, raunchy cigar hidden out of goat's reach along with a butane lighter. I lit the smelly thing and puffed on it to get a good imitation of Mount St. Helens going and held it in my hand between two fingers. Then, while the fear was still in his face, I cupped the lit end over his nose while cradling the back of his head with his chin up, in my other arm. The ember of the cigar was too far away to burn his nose, but the natural response to having his nose covered suddenly was to inhale deeply. When the smoke filled his lungs, he lurched back and started coughing. He didn't know what hit him. All he knew was he didn't like it. This may seem cruel but it really isn't: If he became a "butt and run" goat, he'd have to be destroyed. Such behavior is simply not acceptable in a working animal. The beauty of my method is that, if it's used in a timely fashion it only needs to be used once. That was the first and last time T.C. ever butted me, and for nine more years he was one of my all-around best packers.

Now, if T.C. even mildly gets that Clint Eastwood look in his eyes or tries anything else he knows he shouldn't, I have only to say his name in the same tone of voice I used just before applying the cigar therapy and he straightens right out. If anyone shows up on the trail or at home smoking anything at all, T.C. instantly becomes a lovable little 250-pound munchkin with a silly expression that says, "Aren't I cute?"

I've used this method on two other late-cut wethers and a horse I was breaking with the same successful results—and I only had to do it once in each case. The method works best if you apply it the *first* time an animal attempts an unacceptable stunt.

Another method of applying nonviolent surprise is the old squirt-gun trick. Keep a small water pistol handy when working with a potential problem animal. A shot of water in the face at just the right time is very effective. For more serious offenders, put a drop or two of ammonia in the water for a repulsive smell. And to really leave a lasting impression, put a small amount of "eau de goat" (filtered tea made from boiled goat raisins) into the squirt gun. A little bit goes a long way!

A technique useful for less serious offenses is simply to bend over and let a sudden burst of air out of your mouth close to the goat's nose. This should sound like a goat sneeze, which is very similar to the warning snort that is intelligible to all caprids and extremely startling to them. These surprise negative stimuli generally do not result in attempts at retribution.

On the trail, late-cut wethers are usually not at all aggressive because much of their excess energy is used up working. But if you do see that look in an individual's eye, give him an extra 10 pounds to carry the next day. Working goats tend to be very agreeable animals. If they are working really hard, extra grain will give them extra energy; the excess energy is directed toward working and away from mischief. Thus, if they are *not* working hard, extra grain will make them potentially mischievous. Regulate their grain ration according to need.

Mischief or any other bad habits your goat may exhibit should be treated with the negative reinforcements described. Chasing, beating, shouting, or any display of emotion on your part wastes your energy, is ineffective in the long run, and may end up becoming a "bad habits game" you play with increasing frequency as soon as your goat realizes he's getting *your* goat!

Mischief is a common method of expressing yourself if you are a goat—a way of expending the great surplus of caprine energy that well-fed goats seem to develop. This is the same energy you are tapping when, under your guidance, your goat is working for you. You must judiciously guide the mischief as well as the energy, because there will always be mischief. Because it is so cute in a young animal, people often unknowingly encourage it as the animal grows, allowing it to flourish and mature into what can become a devastating caprice. Believe me! These are things I had to learn the hard way, and they *are* preventable.

The Games Goats Play could be the subject of an entire book. Here is a common scenario: You catch your loyal compadre sticking his nose under the pack cover draped over the food panniers. You dash over, screaming at him, as he is about to taste a bagel. You grab his collar, slap him with your hand, and kick at him a few times. He runs off. The next time, he sneaks in on tiptoes, and by the time you notice him, he's got the bagel in his mouth. But this time he runs off with it when you approach, screaming. You chase him but can't catch him. The *next* time, he sneaks in and sneaks out with the whole bag of bagels undetected, but you hit him when you discover the caper.

A year later you find yourself getting out of the sleeping bag on a beautiful glacier, five days from the nearest trailhead, with the sun rising in a clear blue sky. Life couldn't be much better. The goats are lazily perched in the nearby rocks in a life-sized mural of pastoral innocence framed by sky and snow. But when you arrive at the food panniers, to your surprise they're empty except for two cans of olives and a jar of horseradish. After following the tracks left in the midnight snow, you find all the food bags dropped in rock crevices, many crunched by caprine hooves, but nothing eaten. Outraged, you yell *his* name, and from the surrounding peaks the echo returns, sounding like a distraught forty-year-old Heidi yodeling "GOATIUS MAXIMUS! Get your *!*!* over here!"

Ol' Goatius, of course, is innocently headed for one of those peaks where he knows you can't catch him, wearing a smile of satisfaction for yet another victory in the battle between the species.

There is no question about it, whether it's people or goats, the game is always more fun if the risks are high. Drug smugglers, gunrunners, and soldiers of fortune rarely do it for the money alone. It's the thrill of beating the odds when the risks are high. It's the game that's important. And who sets the rules for this game? I'll give you one guess—and Goatius Maximus is not the right answer. Goats are not born with a lot of game plans in their genes. The games must be learned, and caprids are fast learners who don't forget for a long time. If goats were truly discouraged by pain and discomfort, they wouldn't go around beating their heads against one another. That is just another game—one that *is* written in their genes— where the risk is pain and discomfort and the payoff is dominance.

But while pain is a risk programmed into the C.C. (caprine computer) as part of the game plan, shame is not. At least shame seems to be processed a little differently, especially when it is passed down from the "Supreme Goat" (that's you, if your goats were bottle-fed and trained by you), and when it occurs as a totally unprogrammed surprise—the squirt gun with water, ammonia, or goat manure sprayed on his body; a blast of air blown in his nose with an alarm noise; or smoke in his lungs—he understands he's been outwitted. You won't retrain your goat with brute force, but you might by jamming his computer!

■11■
Acquiring and Keeping Goats: Home Sweet Home

ONCE YOU HAVE DECIDED THAT PACK GOATS ARE FOR YOU, you have two options. Many folks who have access to a pack-goat farm will prefer the low-cost "rent-a-goat" approach. If you don't have any land, or you travel a lot, or you need a goat for only one week a year, well, renting is cheaper and more practical than owning a goat. If, on the other hand, you like the idea of enjoying the companionship of a relatively expressive and intelligent animal and/or have the facilities to keep one or two on a year-round basis, you may choose to make a purchase and become a goat-keeper.

Keeping goats entails some responsibility. As with keeping any other animal, being responsible implies first being knowledgeable about your animals, their needs, and your ability to fill those needs.

There are several good books on goat-keeping listed in the Selected Reading, and you will probably want to refer to them as well as read this chapter and get some insights from other local goat owners. The books, of course, concentrate on the female of the species because they are written for people who want to have milk goats. If you plan to keep a doe with your wether(s), I strongly suggest you read some of these books first. If you plan only to have wether goats, you should still read these for the

117

Photograph courtesy of Gail Schilling

general information on goats. But be aware that keeping wethers is much easier than keeping does once you are set up for it. Basically, in order to keep goats, you must provide: land; shelter; food, water, and health care; and companionship.

The ideal land setup would be several acres of shrubby rangeland with a spring and a cliff. This is hard to come by for most folks, but if you live near such a place, don't fail to inquire about it. Wethers can browse noxious weeds and overcrowding scrub growth from horse pastures and cow pastures, thus doing a service to the landowner by improving his land's grazing potential. For instance, goats have been used in Wyoming, Montana, and other states to control leafy spurge, a pretty little forb that is a delicacy and highly nutritious for goats, but very poisonous to almost every other life form. Goats are also occasionally put on sheep pastures to protect sheep from predators. You may be able to make a trade with the landowner or allotment holder. This last option is really the best, because sheep fencing will often hold goats if it is high enough.

If the allotment is large enough, a fence isn't necessary, because goats will find their niche and stake out their home range in a rather small habitat. An area with a one-mile radius, a good variety of plants, a constant water supply, and climbing rocks or a hill for his itchy feet will satisfy a goat's habitat requirements. You should walk the range with your goats to establish their movement patterns. These patterns will last a lifetime if the habitat satisfies all their needs. I walked my unfenced open rangeland with my lead doe, her kids, and one wether twenty years ago. We saw the spring, the cliff, the mile or so of sagebrush steppe, and the pine and aspen groves leading back to my cabin. Though all of those original animals are long gone, my present herd, descended from them, still travels almost those exact footsteps every day. And because they all come to the sound of a special bell, roundups are easy and quick.

The presence of these goats over a long period of time has actually made a noticeable improvement in the growth and availability of the grasses eaten by the cows that also occupy this range. Everyone benefits. This kind of balanced range management could greatly increase livestock production and decrease management costs (for instance in weed control) in this country if it were ever put into common practice. But that's the subject of another book!

On government range allotments in the West, you can look into trading AUMs (animal unit months—a standard measure of a species' relative utilization of a habitat that is used by government management agencies) with an existing grazing association or private lease-holder. (The Government Printing Office in Washington, D.C., offers Bureau of Land Management publications that contain scientific information on the use of goats for balancing rangeland plant communities and improving grazing land for cows and horses.)

Maybe you have a small piece of land. Check the local ordinances and covenants to make sure goats are allowed. If so, you need a fence to keep your neighbors from becoming your enemies. The fence can be wood or wire, and ideally should be 5 feet high. A 4-1/2- or 5-foot fence is usually adequate, but some wethers are incredible jumpers and require a higher fence. It all depends on the individual animal. One jumper in the crowd can teach a whole herd of nonjumpers how to clear a 4-1/2-foot fence, but rarely a 5-foot fence. Four feet of woven wire (field fence) with two strands of unbarbed wire above is a good combination. Some people have had good success with three or five strands of electric fence, but all the occupants of a yard so enclosed must be trained (shocked) before it will work well. And don't forget that your fence may have to play more of a role in keeping out your neighbor's dogs than keeping your goats in.

Chain link or woven wire fence is relatively easy to put up. The posts should be 8 to 12 feet apart and securely set in the ground. All corners should be braced to keep the wire from sagging when the goats stand on it. Sometimes kids will tend to stick their heads through the squares in woven wire and get their horns stuck, requiring a rescue on your part. If this becomes a repeated occurrence, you may want to put some temporary flashing from the ground up to a height of about 3 feet until their horns grow out (usually at about 10 months). Some people disbud (remove horn buds with heat or caustic paste) their kids for just this purpose. If you also have small children and are worried about accidents, well, you may want to do this anyway. The decision is yours.

Make your fence tight and free of weak spots, low spots, and holes, and you will be able to keep goats in. True, goats are legendary escape artists. Some folks say you can't fence a goat in, but escapes always trace back to a defect in the fence. Goats seem to possess some mystical power to spot an unseen weakness in a fence and, when no one is looking, escape without a trace. Remember that goats will stand on fences, and if the fence is not strong enough, it will sag or even get pushed over in places—and there go the goats!

My favorite story of how to build a goat-tight fence was told to me by a friend who had some (at least conjectural) experience with goats. It goes like this: First build a solid wooden fence about 10 feet high to completely enclose a flat paddock. Make sure you can't see any light through the boards. Then go outside the fence you just built and build another fence exactly like the first 3 feet away from it. When it's completed, fill the 3-foot space between the two fences with concrete up to 10 feet and let it set. Finally, fill the entire paddock enclosure with water to the 10-foot level. If it holds water, it'll probably hold goats!

Now that you have an enclosure, let's look at what's in it. Not any ornamental trees or shrubs, I hope. They will be the first to be eaten. Any plants you want to save must be fenced off. Remember, goats are more browsers than grazers.

If you have a large pasture, determine whether the vegetation will support your animals or if you will need to feed them supplemental feed. If supplemental feed is needed, or if you own just a small plot of land such as a backyard, you will need a hay shed that will hold at least a ton of hay (alfalfa, grass, sweet-clover, or mixed)—it's cheaper by the ton. A shed 8 feet by 10 feet by 8 feet will easily hold a ton of hay with enough extra space for some tools, vet supplies, a grain barrel (55-gallon drum full of COB), and so on. Figure on feeding a little over a ton of hay to one goat per year if you have a small pasture. With a large pasture containing good goat feed, you may not have to feed any hay, but you should always keep some around for emergencies, or to boost the quality of pasture feed in winter and in spring during the growth surge.

Attached to the hay shed, if possible, should be the goat lodging. The two buildings, or one divided building, should be separated so that there is no chance your innocent-looking little friend can gain entry into the hay shed and ruin your hay. Goats like to climb up on hay stacks and "hang out." Their bodily functions do not cease while the goats are hanging out, and since goats detest the presence of goat droppings or urine on anything they might eat or drink, one goat need spend only a few nights in the hay shed to destroy a half-ton of fine alfalfa. Furthermore, the grain barrel must be secure. Goats can founder on too much grain, just as horses can.

A shed for wethers should be small. A small shed will contain body heat better in winter and on cold nights. The minimum area needed is 2 feet by 4 feet per goat—4 feet by 4 feet is probably better and borders on palatial. If you have more than five goats, at least one divider should be installed to separate high-ranking from low-ranking members of the pecking order.

The roof should be 5 to 6 feet high in front, should slope gently toward the back for drainage, and should incorporate a 2-foot overhang in front. It should be covered with 90-pound rolled roofing. The shed can be open in front if it faces away from storm winds as well as prevailing winds. If dogs or other predators are a potential problem, or if the winter climate is particularly harsh, a small entryway is preferred to an open front. The opening should be about 2 feet wide by 3 feet high. If you have divided cubicles, each must have its own entryway. Dogs or coyotes are not likely to pursue goats through a constricted passageway like this because horned goats have the obvious advantage in head-to-head confrontations.

If your animals have no other high point to play on, the shed roof can be covered with mortared slab rock or concrete and made accessible with a 3-foot-high bench or rock behind the shed. The rock or concrete roof will keep the goats' hooves trimmed and also toughen the soft parts of the hoof.

A hay-feeding, or supplemental-feeding, program should include a manger or feed trough, either inside the shed in wet climates or free-standing outside the shed. Just dropping hay on the ground is wasteful, unsanitary, and generally not a good practice. A manger can be constructed easily inside the shed by installing a trough 8 inches wide by 8 inches deep and 2 feet off the ground along one of the side walls. Rough lumber, 2-by-8, works well for this. Dividers should be installed at 10- to 12-inch intervals to keep the goats separated while feeding and to keep large flakes of hay from being pulled out onto the floor. Wooden or welded-wire fencing with 4- to 6-inch-square openings (often called "hog panels" or "cattle panels") will both work well as dividers, although there is less waste of hay with the wire type.

"Keyhole" mangers are often used for hornless goats. The keyhole is simply a round hole about 10 to 12 inches in diameter cut into a plywood wall, with a 6- to 8-inch-wide slot cut from the hole down about a foot to the trough. The hay is behind the wall. The feeding goat's neck is held in place by the slot as long as he is feeding, but he is free to lift his head and pull out of the hole at any time. Keyholes are common with hornless herds.

There are many styles of manger and many disputes over which is best. Some of the goat books listed in the Selected Reading will give you other options, particularly for hornless goats. Because goats like clean feed and will not eat hay that has fallen to the ground and been trampled, an efficient manger will reduce your annual feed cost considerably.

You can save time by cutting a slot in the shed wall above the manger that is large enough to allow you to throw in flakes of hay from the outside; this way you won't have to fight off the goat feeding frenzy that would occur were you to load the manger from inside. An opening 2 feet by 3 feet will be sufficient. This slot should be fitted with a hinged door that pulls down to open.

A bit of shrub and grass pasture with a good mix of forbs (broad-leaved weeds), and a regular alfalfa or sweet-clover supplement is the ideal way to keep pack wethers. How much land is enough? Well, that's impossible to say without knowing the type and condition of vegetation and its year-round availability. In very arid, sparse land, it may take three acres or more to support a goat. In more lush habitats, one-half acre per goat may be enough. Supplemental alfalfa for calcium and protein is a good idea, along with a supplemental grain mix for phosphorus, additional protein, and training purposes.

Feeding and caring for pack wethers is generally a much easier prospect than feeding and caring for breeding goats. If you plan to get into a breeding operation, you need to read a few books on dairy goats and study up on that technology before jumping into it. There are many more things to be concerned with once you pass that threshold. With wethers, however, especially those bred and raised for packing, the job is far less complicated.

Here are some pointers: Wethers are healthier and happier with lots of fiber in their diet. Willow, poplar, cottonwood, aspen, pine, fir, spruce— in fact, most trees and shrubs are better for your wether than a steady diet of grass. In most areas, these woody foods are available on at least a seasonal basis and are usually *free*. Tree trimmers, tree surgeons, county or city street and road maintenance crews, and some city recycling yards often have surplus woody vegetation that you can haul off after getting approval from the appropriate authority. If you think you don't have a source in your area, think again. Christmas-tree vendors often dump hundreds of cut trees that don't get sold by December 24. You can make prior arrangements to save some tree dealer a trip to the dump and haul off trailer loads of good feed. If you decide to pick up "used" trees or leftover trees from the lot after Christmas, you need to be discriminating. Don't take trees with dry needles, tinsel, metal ornament hangers, flocking, artificial coloring, or fire retardant. You can hurt your wether with these things. I feed my goats Christmas trees every year from December to March (with supplemental alfalfa/grain and pasture), and the leftover peeled sticks (the goats don't leave much!) are used up in the wood stove to heat my house.

Some goat owners have been concerned about too much pine in the diet causing abortions in pregnant does. This fear comes from cattle country, where eating some long-needled pines, such as ponderosa or torrey pine, causes abortion in cows. I've never seen this happen in goats. Remember, goats eat trees and shrubs for a living; cows don't.

Although supplemental COB (corn, oats, and barley) is necessary for the proper growth and bone development of a pack wether, the need decreases as the animal's growth rate decreases. Chronologically speaking, for maximum growth, a kid should be allowed to have milk as a primary diet until it's at least three months of age. After that, weanlings (freshly weaned wethers) should be given up to 1/4-pound of grain a day and a bit more during spring green-up when the annual growth spurt is on. This should be continued to age two, then reduced to 1/4-pound every second day until age five, when bone growth essentially stops. The exception is in springtime, when the annual growth spurt can be enhanced by a daily dose of grain—for protein and phosphorus—for about a month.

After they are five years old, wethers can be taken off grain altogether, except for an occasional handout, treat, or reward during training. Too much phosphorus after age five, especially when associated with a high-calcium diet, can have deleterious effects on mature wethers, particularly during inactive periods in the off-season. It can lead to urinary calculi (bladder stones) and/or changes in disposition, including neurotic or even aggressive behavior.

Regularly freshened does (does having kids every year) are not affected by these levels of phosphorus because they can shunt it into the milk supply. Wethers that are working hard will also utilize both excess phosphorus and protein without harmful effects.

During the springtime growth phase, a high-protein alfalfa should make up at least fifty percent of a wether's daily intake (2 to 4 pounds dry weight, depending on the weight of the animal). This can be reduced to twenty percent the rest of the year, including winter in the northern latitudes, when woody, high-cellulose plants such as willows and other members of the poplar family will actually produce more metabolic body heat than will high-protein feeds. If only hay is available, wethers more than four years old should have a 50/50 mixture of alfalfa and a quality hay grass, like orchard grass, timothy, or brome. Stay away from crested wheatgrass in hay.

In Saanens and Toggs, the critical growth period for wethers is the spring of the first year. In Alpines and Oberhaslis it is the spring of the second year. Illness or poor feeding programs at these critical times can permanently stunt your wether's growth. If he's going to be carrying a load, this is not fair to him or to you. Feeding limbs from trees that have been sprayed for Dutch elm disease or other insects or fungi can also stunt his growth, as well as make him sick, so take all the necessary steps to be certain everything you feed your hiking buddy is safe. You'll usually find that lawn-mowing leftovers are not safe or even nutritious for your wether, so it's a good policy to turn down offers of free grass piles, even though such offers can be a heavy temptation. Lawn clippings and similar refuse also can contain bits of broken glass or metal fragments that can seriously injure a goat.

This leads us to our final concern in keeping a pack goat—health. In general, goats are remarkably healthy and resilient animals. Wethers that get exercise regularly are *exceptionally* healthy as a rule. This doesn't mean they won't get sick from time to time. If you are new to goat-keeping, there are several things you should do to ensure the health of your charge.

First, try to acquire your goat from a reputable dairy or pack-goat breeder. Both will have taken the necessary precautions to see that their animals are in good shape. Pack-goat breeders will be especially mindful of the maladies that can cause you problems down the road. Since many goat diseases are regional phenomena, a conscientious breeder will already have taken care of the vaccinations, mineral supplements, or special precautions necessary for his or her area, and probably can give you a few good hints for future health maintenance.

Second, pick up one or several of the books and magazines listed in the Selected Reading and read the sections on disease and veterinary care. This will give you an overview of what to look for, and will list some emergency treatments.

Third, get to know your local veterinarian. If you have a choice, look for one who knows goats (not all vets do). And do this *before* an emergency comes up. Bring your wether in for a checkup, and once every year thereafter have your vet look at him before the packing season begins. There are several reasons for this. One important reason is to appease those people who believe goats are dirty animals that will bring disease into the backcountry and kill off all the wild animals. In fact, goats are exceptionally clean animals, but most people don't realize this. So it sometimes helps to have a veterinary health certificate to show (if for no other reason) that you're concerned about wildlife—and about your pack animal.

Commercial packers should do this voluntarily every year. The cost is minimal, and it shows in good faith that you care about the backcountry —which you should anyway, if you're going to use it.

Unlikely as it is that you'll have a serious health problem in a working wether, there are a wide variety of ailments that can affect a goat (as you will see by thumbing through the vet section of any book on goat husbandry). I've listed a few of the more common health problems you should be prepared for with working wethers.

C.A.E. (Caprine arthritis and encephalitis). This is a serious viral infection that is passed from dam to kid by way of the milk. Thousands of goats have died from this disease since its discovery in the early 1980s. Prevention involves simply pasteurizing the milk of an infected doe before feeding it to the kids. A blood test can identify exposure to the virus. Symptoms vary, but generally the animal will be lethargic and show swelling of the joints, particularly the front knee joints. If your goat definitely has C.A.E., the best thing to do is put him down, because sometime during his prime (between two and five years old) he will most likely become feeble, deformed, and unpackable—not to mention being in a lot of pain. Packgoat breeders are usually very careful to have completely C.A.E.-free herds, and are proud to tell you so. But because C.A.E. is still common in North America, you should ask about it when you buy a wether, and have a blood test done if the answer is uncertain. A pack goat with C.A.E. is not worth the investment in training and bonding.

Because it's a new disease, there is still much discussion about C.A.E. and its transmission. But strict pasteurization of kid milk is having a direct and very positive effect on curtailing the incidence of C.A.E., which was once out of control. A similar disease exists in sheep but is caused by a different organism. The two infections are thought to be species-specific and are not transmissible between sheep and goats.

Caseous lymphadenitis. This is a contagious, debilitating disease resulting in periodic outbreaks of lumps under the skin ranging from golfball to baseball size. These lumps eventually break and produce an ooze the consistency of cottage cheese ("caseous" means cheeselike). This ooze contaminates the ground, fences, and buildings where the goat lives and can thereby infect other goats even long after the originally infected goat is gone. Goats with this disease cannot work because they become lethargic and mentally slow for long periods of time. Training is impossible. No goat with caseous lymphadenitis should ever be sold as a pack animal or brought in contact with working goats, because one animal can ruin an entire herd.

Similar lumps can occur for other reasons that are not serious or contagious. Most abscesses, for instance, are not a problem for goats. So have

your vet investigate any suspicious lump, and have him show you what to look for.

Hardware poisoning. This is a common term for the effects of eating bits of metal, which goats are most likely to pick up off the ground. Pieces of baling wire, small brads or tacks, or any other tiny metallic artifacts of civilization can lodge in and perforate one of the esophageal chambers or the true stomach of any ruminant. So it is imperative that you keep a clean pen, pasture, and shed. Besides being debilitating, hardware poisoning can be difficult to diagnose and can lead to a slow, painful death.

Just because you keep your goats healthy and well cared for, don't forget that diseases can be introduced from other goats or even from wild animals. So if you purchase a new goat or keep someone else's goat with yours for a while, you may be exposing your goat to exotic organisms that could infect him. Most commonly transmitted by contact are eye infections and lung infections; ectoparasites, such as lice and mites; and endoparasites, such as worms.

Through their uniquely playful habits and their affectionate ways with people, goats can bring a good deal of joy to a person's life, as well as function as a faithful pack animal—as long as they are healthy. And good health is something any person can give his goats with just a little study and a watchful eye.

▪12▪
On the Technical Side: Historical Notes

THE GOAT WAS DOMESTICATED ABOUT TEN THOUSAND YEARS ago, five thousand years before the horse. In fact, the archeological evidence indicates that the domestication of the goat predates that of all other animals, with the possible exception of the dog. All of the known wild goats, as well as many wild sheep, are curious about man's activities in the wild and are easily domesticated. Partly because of the long period of time involved, there is some confusion over the domestic goat's point of origin both geographically and as a species.

No one really knows which goat was first taken from the wild to live with humans. Some experts believe the earliest archeological evidence lies in caves in Turkey and Greece. There is evidence that a second line of goat probably emerged in North Africa. There is evidence for yet another line coming from the foothills of the Himalayas. All these wild progenitors of the goat are separate species according to our present taxonomy, and not all have living representatives today.

The wild goats commonly accepted as the progenitors of present-day domestic goats are: the wild goat or bezoar (*Capra aegagrus*), sometimes called "pashang," once common throughout the Middle East; the Spanish ibex (*Capra pyrenaica*) of the Pyrenees; the markhor (*Capra falconeri*),

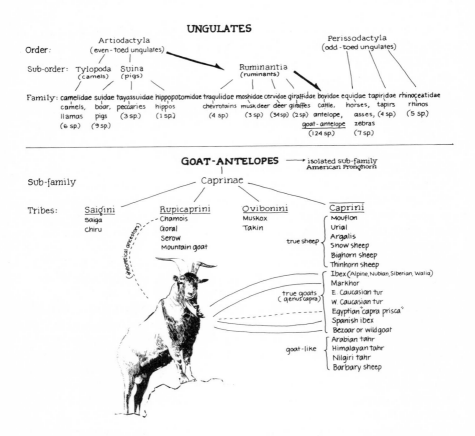

UNGULATES

Order:	Artiodactyla (even-toed ungulates)										Perissodactyla (odd-toed ungulates)		
Sub-order:	Tylopoda (camels)	Suina (pigs)				Ruminantia (ruminants)							
Family:	camelidae	suidae	tayassuidae	hippopotomidae	traqulidae	moshidae	cervidae	giraffidae	bovidae	equidae	tapiridae	rhinoceatidae	
	camels,	boar,	peccaries	hippos	chevrotains	muskdeer	deer	giraffes	cattle,	horses,	tapirs	rhinos	
	llamas	pigs	(3 sp.)	(1 sp.)	(4 sp.)	(3 sp.)	(34sp.)	(2 sp.)	antelope,	asses,	(4 sp.)	(5 sp.)	
	(6 sp.)	(9 sp.)							goat-antelope	zebras			
									(124 sp.)	(7 sp.)			

GOAT-ANTELOPES → isolated sub-family American Pronghorn

Sub-family — Caprinae

Tribes:

Saigini	Rupicaprini	Ovibonini	Caprini
Saiga	Chamois	Muskox	Mouflon
Chiru	Goral	Takin	Urial
	Serow		Argalis
	Mountain goat		Snow sheep } true sheep
			Bighorn sheep
			Thinhorn sheep

(theoretical ancestry)

true goats (genus capra)
- Ibex (Alpine, Nubian, Siberian, Walia)
- Markhor
- E. Caucasian tur
- W. Caucasian tur
- Egyptian 'capra prisca'
- Spanish ibex
- Bezoar or wildgoat

goat-like
- Arabian tahr
- Himalayan tahr
- Nilgiri tahr
- Barbary sheep

a spiral-horned goat of central Asia; and *Capra prisca,* theorized to have lived in North Africa.

These are sophisticated guesses based primarily on similarities between wild goats and those domestic goats thought to have originated in the same general vicinity with them. My own observations along these lines have led me to suspect two other species sources: a now-extinct Siberian relative of the Siberian ibex (*Capra ibex sibirica*), and the Swiss chamois (*Rupicapra rupicapra*), currently living in the Alps. This last will raise a few eyebrows in scientific circles, because the chamois is a very distant and primitive relative of the domestic goat. In fact, the chamois is not a true goat at all, but a goat-antelope. My reasoning for these suspicions comes in part from information that was not apparent until the various goat breeds were subjected to the rigors of becoming "beasts of burden." You can learn quite a lot about your hiking partner by how he performs under a heavy pack on a warm day.

Each breed of goat has its own tendencies, along with the usual array of exceptions to the rule, but knowing breed tendencies will help you select the right goat for the job. And knowing the wild origins of these breeds will help you understand these tendencies.

Caprids, especially goat-antelopes, are some of the earliest ruminant animals to occur in the fossil record. The living representatives of this group today show tremendous variation in their physical appearances and adaptations. One way to explain this variation is based on the known abilities of these animals today. For instance, goats like rock. So do almost all other caprids. In fact, *Rupicapra,* the chief genus in the goat-antelope group, means "rock goat." Goats feel most comfortable on exposed, windy cliff faces with sparse vegetation. Most show an adaptability to periodic dry spells and exposure to extreme cold; others, to extreme heat. Some show a tolerance for both extreme heat *and* extreme cold. Goats are also famous for acute long-distance vision.

What conditions would select for just this combination of traits? The answer is tricky because it's a place that exists in a constant state of flux, a place that's constantly moving. It is the edge of a glacier.

Ice ages alternately have enveloped the northern hemisphere of this planet, then receded, leaving behind a freshly scoured landscape that almost immediately begins rebuilding its fertility. It's a long process—thousands of years long. The slowest places to recover are in the cooler climates found in high mountains. These places are steep, rocky, cold, windy, and sparsely vegetated but abundant in tiny, clean, cool mountain streams freshly melted from remnant ice packs. This is the home of the earliest forms of wild goat.

These places lack the fast-growing grassy savannahs and warm woodlands of the lowlands and deep valleys that are so lush in greenery. But the apparently hostile environment of the rocky mountainside has an advantage over the productive low country. All that productivity attracts large numbers of animals in huge herds, which in turn attract large numbers of predators that terrorize the herds daily. To escape a predator, an herbivore must outrun it or get lost in the crowd. It's only a matter of time before a particular herbivore becomes prey.

Although predators live in the craggy parts of mountain ranges, a sure-footed herbivore has an advantage. It can escape to a ledge or a cave and wait out the threat. In many wild habitats, the eagle is actually the most effective wild predator of wild goats and sheep because it is able to pick young kids and lambs off ledges that are inaccessible to other predators.

These lofty rock edifices are not obscured by tall vegetation or under-growth. The bare rock stands majestically in plain view, with neighboring mountainsides and peaks often miles apart. Here, farsightedness is of greater advantage than knowing how to follow your nose. Caprids, including domestic goats, can see seven times farther than humans. Walking with one is like wearing a pair of binoculars.

The young, fragile soils of postglacial mountains generally don't support large expanses of grassy meadow. Instead, hardy, woody forms of shrubs and forbs are dominant and more available above winter snows. Caprids adapted by showing a preference for tough, woody plant species of all kinds. To this day, domestic goats are used to clear shrub lands in preparation for other land uses such as farming, tree plantations, and firebreaks.

The digestion of extremely high-fiber woody plants requires a special-ized system of masticating plant materials, dunking them in fluids laced with acids and enzymes, then chewing again, followed by more dousing in corrosive liquids. This process is repeated several times before the final phase of nutrient extraction occurs. This is why goats chew their "cud" (a wad of partially digested plant material). All animals that chew cud are ruminants—animals with specialized digestive tracts that feature enlarged areas, in addition to the true stomach, that selectively process food in stages, sending it back up periodically for chewing.

Often goats can be seen lying in the sun, eyes half-closed, chewing away at a steady rate for hours in pure caprine bliss. If you look closely at their throats, you can actually see the lump that is the cud being swallowed and new cud being regurgitated up into the mouth to be chewed again. Goats produce a large number of digestive enzymes as well as microorganisms that produce other enzymes. All these enzymes not only enable the breakdown of extremely coarse, fibrous materials containing cellulose but also denature many plant poisons designed to protect the plant from being eaten. The advantages of this complex process for an animal living where vegetation is scarce are obvious.

The goat-antelope, like the chamois and Rocky Mountain goat, were the earliest life forms on earth to chew their cud. They were followed by true goats, sheep, antelope, and cattle. But of all these, the goats achieved the highest level of diversity in the types of plants they could digest. "They seem to be able to eat anything," is a common description. There are instances of goats living on nothing but cardboard boxes for weeks at a time. This is certainly not a recommended diet, but under emer-gency circumstances, it works.

As glacial remnants receded, early wild goats gradually expanded their range higher up the mountain to exploit the newly emerging environments. They eventually developed a thick coat of hair (especially adapted to dry out quickly after being dampened) and a physiological adaptation to extremely cold, windy climates. Descended from these animals, the hair goats of the Middle East and Central Asia are famous for their cold-tolerance, and their hair—mohair and cashmere, respectively—is notoriously warm when made into clothing, and soft and quick to dry when wet. This last characteristic explains why mohair historically has been the material of choice for horse-saddle cinches.

After thousands of years of alpine living, these wild goats adapted perfectly to a specialized niche. But sometime after these adaptations were firmly in place, the earth's climate once again changed and, slowly, ice and snow moved down the mountains and south across continents, forcing our happily adjusted goats into new lands. Some would relocate into mountainous areas for which they were already adapted. Others, in southern locations unaffected by the new ice age, did not need to move. But others were forced to lower elevations where they were vulnerable prey to a large contingent of predators. Small groups of these animals made the adjustment, however, by finding rocky terrain for escape cover in new climates.

In time the glaciers again receded, and isolated small populations of goats were then required to adapt to ever-warming temperatures and drying conditions. Over thousands of years, many goats adapted to desert climates; examples are the Nubian ibex (*Capra ibex nubiana*), ranging from the Arabian Peninsula to the Ethiopian deserts, and the rare walia ibex (*Capra walie*) of the mountains of western Ethiopia, which rarely if ever drinks water, even though surrounded by flowing streams, preferring to derive its water from the plants it eats. Other goats instead followed the receding ice back up to the mountaintops. Thousands more years passed, and a new ice age repeated the process all over again.

By now enough time had passed that adaptation and isolation caused separated populations to look and act differently in some ways, but *not* enough time had passed to prevent crossbreeding in these divergent forms, called "racial clines." This means that when the goats of the high mountains were slowly pushed back to the lowlands, some formerly separated "clines" met and successfully interbred, mingling the gene pools of desert-adapted and alpine-adapted populations. The cyclic tide of glaciation recurred dozens of times, spinning off a wide variety of both desert and mountain (Palearctic) forms, as well as many hybrid forms that have the capacity to endure both extremes.

The need to survive ever-changing environments, from desert bluffs subject to drought-stricken periods of water and food scarcity to 12,000-foot snowy peaks at the edge of the ice pack, endowed these hybrids with very special attributes. Written into the genetic makeup of these animals are the abilities to efficiently recycle urea and thus conserve water in times of drought; to extend the "range of thermoneutrality," that is, to adjust the body's operating temperature (more than any other hooved animal is able to do) as a means of physiologically tolerating a wide variety of climatic conditions; to produce a heavy coat of hair in extremely cold climates while using large porous horns filled with blood vessels like radiators —to dissipate heat in extremely hot climates; to pant like a dog and sweat like a horse as additional heat-releasing methods; to eat and digest the sparse sedges and lichens of alpine crags as well as the thorny bushes, too coarse to be eaten by other animals, growing on sparsely vegetated escarpments of parched salt scrub deserts.

In addition to the above adaptations, goats have had to develop an adventurous and opportunistic attitude toward exploration when food and water resources were few and far between. This tendency to peer around every boulder and check out anything new and different-looking has given the goat the reputation of being the most curious hooved animal on earth.

Stories of wild goats, and caprids in general, walking right up to people in the wild who are behaving somehow abnormally are common around the globe. I personally have experienced this trait in the mountains and in the desert on many occasions. It becomes clear after the first encounter of this kind why goats and sheep were the first domesticated herbivores. It's an old Indian trick to lure a pronghorn antelope (colloquially called "goats" in Wyoming) to the kill by waving a rag on the end of a stick from behind a boulder. Just out of curiosity, I've lured both pronghorn antelope (actually an early goat-antelope) and bighorn sheep this way. Domestic goats in the wild are just as curious. Once you have one domesticated caprid, he or she, often called a "Judas goat," will serve as the most effective lure of other caprids, of the same or different species. When you know this, it's clear that wild goats and sheep were destined to become domesticated long before other hooved animals.

It is also clear that the goat is among the oldest types of hooved animals still living. Its position as the chief colonizer of the interglacial mountain zone, constantly subject to this zone's ups and downs of climate and degree of hospitableness, has given us a unique animal, and one of tremendous flexibility.

Not all domestic goats today have this same adaptive makeup. The domestic goat had its origins in at least four different places (and probably more than that). These areas ranged from the Pyrenees in Western Europe to the Himalayas, and probably Mongolia, in the Far East. Most domestic goats first appeared at about the same time, around nine thousand to ten thousand years ago.

The bezoar still lives on steep slopes and crags in the Middle East. It is a species capable of a wide range of adaptability, and is the one living ancestor that most domestic goats seem to resemble most closely. Its traits

Bezoar (Capra aegagrus)

are most clearly seen in Toggenburg, Saanen, and, to a lesser degree, Alpine lines in American breeds, and in many other breeds existing in Europe.

The adult bezoar is large-boned, heavy-legged, and stocky (males may reach 350 pounds). Horns are tan (unpigmented), large, and corrugated, becoming smooth toward the tip. A basal circumference of 30 centimeters is not unusual in the male, while 18 centimeters is typical for the female. The horns are flattened on the inside, curved (scimitar-shaped), 60 to 80 centimeters long in the male and about 30 centimeters in the female. The horn emerges from the head with a slight backward tilt, curves backward and then out with a sharp bend just short of the midway point in males, although not in females.

The body size, build, horn structure, and coat coarseness of the bezoar are so faithfully duplicated in Toggenburgs and Saanens as to make the relationship between them undeniable. The only major difference is in the color of the hair—Toggenburgs are brown with white facial stripes and rump, Saanens are usually pure white. The bezoar is mottled brown, black, gray, and white with facial stripes of various colors. The resemblance is so close that it is possible that the bezoar, instead of being an ancestor of modern domestic goats, actually represents a feral population of goats that escaped domestication thousands of years ago. There is no way to know what the truth of the matter is.*

---

*Goats that become feral often establish very stable populations that, in a few generations, adjust to local conditions and can resemble wild populations in all ways.

Breed Characteristics

The differences between Saanens and Toggenburgs suggest a possible wild ancestor to the Saanen not found in Toggs. It would most likely be an Asian wild goat, perhaps an extinct relative of the Siberian ibex that adapted to high elevations and/or northern latitudes and with white hair and a heavy winter coat, possibly related to the modern Cashmere goat as well.

The Saanen is the largest of the breeds commonly used for packing, but it is also the most susceptible to overheating. As a rule, Saanens are slightly superior to all other breeds under high-alpine wintertime conditions, but they begin to show a lowering of working endurance at temperatures exceeding 80° Fahrenheit, and start panting with moderate working stress somewhere between 80° and 95°, depending on the individual. These reactions are even more severe in high humidity. (High humidity lowers the working performance of almost any animal, but especially goats.) Toggs, although not as heat-tolerant as Alpines or LaManchas, are much more heat-tolerant than Saanens.

For these reasons, if you need a pack goat for the jungles of southern Mexico or the desert around Tucson, Arizona, the Saanen is not a good choice. If, however, you plan on spending your summers in the 12,000-foot high country of Colorado, Wyoming, or Montana, it is a good choice. These are extreme examples, of course.

The domestic goats of the Alps were brought in to that area by the earliest human settlers as an efficient source of milk in alpine terrain. It's apparent that these animals represent a mix of Middle Eastern milk, meat, and hair goats that were later selectively bred for high milk production in several isolated regions, yielding isolated breed characteristics such as coat and hide color, milk production, milk butterfat content, and disposition.

The French Alpine, from which the American Alpine goat is derived, is an interesting anomaly. Although the Alpine was originally found in western Switzerland and the French Alps, apparently it descended from the same wild stock as the Saanen and Toggenburg clines. It does show some major differences in structure, physiology, and disposition, though.

The horns (usually a good indicator of bloodlines) of Alpines show an undeniable resemblance to Saanens and Toggs, but they are scaled down both in length and basal circumference and are uniformly of an entirely different color—black instead of tan. From the side, Alpine horns show a slightly anterior (toward-the-nose) tilt. Other traits—such as a long snout, fine bone structure, smaller size, black or mottled black hide (Saanens have pink hides and Toggs gray), more frequent pecking-order disputes, a tendency to be trailwise, a smooth running gait, and the occasional occurrence of extra udder chambers associated with extra teats (at a higher rate of incidence than in other breeds)—suggest to me a more recent injection (hundreds rather than thousands of years ago) of wild goat-antelope stock, specifically, the Swiss or Italian race of chamois, which shows all these characteristics.*

Most striking, however, are the similarities in color patterns between some lines of Alpines and chamois, some of which are almost identical. One of the official Alpine color patterns recognized by the American Dairy Goat Association is called "chamoisee," and is very close to the winter coat of the Swiss chamois. Some of the standard markings found on all registered Alpines are also found on wild chamois. These wild chamois live in the same region in the western Alps in which goatherds have historically run their stock, and it is likely that accidental crossbreedings have occurred many times.

The Oberhasli, a domestic breed used for milk and packing and noted for its beautiful reddish brown coloring, originated largely from French Alpine stock and is colored and marked almost exactly like the summer phase of the Italian chamois. Its horns have an even greater anterior tilt that is very chamoislike in some bloodlines. This, of course, is all circumstantial evidence until more scientific (genetic) research is done. *Rupicapra,* the genus of goat-antelope to which the chamois belongs, is not what taxonomists consider a close relative of the domestic goat. But the nature of interglacial racial clines may allow for just enough genetic similarity for crossbreeding to occur.**

The numerous varieties of Alpine and Oberhasli bloodlines offer special attributes in three main areas: more gracefulness, especially while running; greater "wild"-ness, in the sense of being more "tuned in" to wild environments; and more heat-tolerance than in Saanens and Toggenburgs. Oberhaslis and Alpines also tend to be smaller, with spindly legs, and are slightly less tolerant of extreme cold. But these traits vary widely among the many herds in existence.

In the wild, chamois generally live at lower elevations than do alpine ibex (*Capra ibex*), the true goats native to the same region. Thus, the chamois show adaptations to the gentler terrain and warmer climate of the lower foothills. Chamois are graceful runners in addition to being surefooted. They can run at sustained high speeds in a straight line without the jerky up-and-down motions common to the true goats. True goats run more capriciously, rarely maintaining a straight line and often stopping to

---

*These goat-antelopes have four teats and four udder chambers, while true goats have only two of each.

**There is some scientific evidence that the crossbreeding of very different-looking and geographically separated caprid species produces live offspring.

Nilgiri tahr
(Hemitragus)

Nubian Ibex
(Capra ibex)

Chamois
(Rupicapra rupicapra)

look around. Chamois are also more tolerant of summer heat, although they are seasonally adapted to the harsh winters of the mountain foothills. If the theory that Alpines and thus Oberhaslis descended from the wild chamois is correct, French Alpines and their kin should show some of these tendencies, and they do, although the degree to which they do varies tremendously from one individual to the next.

The Nubian breed is no relation to the wild Nubian ibex. Rather, it is a composite of Middle Eastern, North African, and Mediterranean domestic goats such as Indian milk goats, the Bedouin goat raised on the Arabian Peninsula primarily for meat, and others whose ancestry is unknown but suggested by some experts as having derived from a hypothetical species called *Capra prisca.*

Capra prisca is theorized to be a desert-adapted isolated racial cline, long separated from the interglacial alpine strains, whose descendants all have long, pendulous, ribbed ears (a heat-dissipating characteristic of many desert animals); a large Roman nose (another desert cooling adaptation associated with sheep); and short hair and heavily pigmented (black) hide, another adaptation to warm, sunny climates.

Sometime after its domestication, it's apparent that at least some of the bloodlines of this race must have been bred to serve as guardian animals. That is, animals that would wake in the night and announce the presence of intruders in the camp. This very likely was the practice in the nomadic Bedouin culture, where the greatest obstacle to one's survival in the desert may have been a neighbor.

Although there are exceptions, Nubians are famous for making goat noises with little provocation. Some lines are as good as guinea fowl at announcing intruders in your front yard. Most goats can be trained to react this way, but it seems to come naturally to many Nubians. Other Nubians are not this way at all. Most Nubians also have a tendency toward laziness, although here again there are many exceptions. Maybe under the tidal influence of hundreds of donkeys, camels, and people nomadically wending their way across the desert the floppy-eared goat would gleefully follow along, but when it's one packer and one packed-up goat, the urge to keep going doesn't seem to overwhelm most Nubians.

Since the Nubian has several bloodlines in its ancestry ranging from North African to Indian, there exists a wide range of variability in this breed. Many Nubians have been used successfully for both packing and harness work. Those progenitors of the Nubian that were kept for meat production lend to many bloodlines a large, sturdy, well-filled-out frame that is well suited to a working animal. With some selection, the Nubian could be a fine pack animal, especially for warm climates. There are some good Nubian packers, but at this time the packing success ratio within the breed is low.

The LaMancha originated in Spain and began a surge in popularity among American dairy-goat breeders in the late 1980s—a trend obviously due in large part to this breed's unique, lovable personality and high level of intelligence. The goat's ancestry appears to be derived from a mix of breeds heavily selected for a combination of earlessness and the characteristically endearing LaMancha personality. LaManchas are now common enough to be acquired as working wethers.

There is little or no evidence in the LaMancha of the Spanish goat recently exterminated from Catalina Island, off the California coast. Those goats, left to free-breed by the Spanish in the sixteenth century, remained until the 1980s as a clue to the appearance and gene pool of the Spanish goat of the days of exploration. The goats on Catalina Island bore a hearty resemblance to the wild Spanish ibex still found in dwindling numbers in the wilderness of the Pyrenees Mountains.

The LaMancha, on the other hand, has a coat, hide, and horns similar to the Nubian's (not like those of an ibex) but with a uniquely studious LaMancha personality that is not at all like the capricious Nubian.

The Nubian, of course, is a desert goat, and perhaps this is the background that provides the LaMancha with its heat-tolerance. At this writing, there are only a handful of LaMancha pack goats in the world. But as

interest in the breed grows, it's becoming apparent that the LaMancha may be the breed of choice for desert performance. They consistently show a high level of endurance and tolerance to heat, drought, and irritability on the part of their hominid (*Homo sapiens*) companions. And they are the easiest of all breeds to train.

There is a broad spectrum of variability within each of the domestic goat breeds. It is likely that each of the common European/American breeds contains small percentages of every other breed, including probably genetic traces of chamois and ibex as a result of accidental crossbreeding in the wild. From this vast gene pool there is a tremendous, mostly untapped, potential for working wethers and does. With a little selective breeding and careful upbringing and training in kidhood, it is easy to see that goats can be the ideal pack animal for an extremely wide variety of tasks and conditions, both commercial and recreational.

Once you have a goat with "the right stuff" genetically, you can monitor his health and nutrition and then spend the time it takes to train and condition him to the job ahead. Then he will gleefully take the load off your back and deliver it to your favorite camping spot, asking only that you share your companionship—a unique and wonderful relationship that may just make the pack goat a hiker's best friend in the wilderness.

Happy Packing.

Selected Reading

Back, Joe. *Horses, Hitches, and Rocky Trails.* Boulder, Colo.: Johnson Books, 1959.

Belanger, Jerry. *Raising Milk Goats the Modern Way.* Pownal, Vt.: Garden Way Publishing, 1975.

Crepin, Joseph. *Le Chevre.* Philo, Calif.: Mountain House Press, 1990.

Dairy Goat Journal. Published monthly by Duck Creek Publications, Inc., W2997 Markert Road, Helenville, Wis. 53137.

De Bairacli-Levy, Juliette. *Herbal Handbook for Farm and Stable.* Emmaus, Pa.: Rodale Press, 1977.

Geist, Valerius. *Mountain Sheep.* Chicago: University of Chicago Press, 1971.

MacKenzie, David. *Goat Husbandry.* London: Faber & Faber, 1981.

National Research Council. *Nutrient Requirements of Goats.* Nutrient Requirements of Domestic Animals, no. 15. Washington, D.C.: National Academy Press, 1981.

United Caprine News. Published monthly by Double Mountain Press, P.O. Drawer A, Rotan, Tex. 79546.

Index

Adaptations, 89–95, 129, 131–33, 136; physiological, 91–92, 130–31, 132

Aggressiveness, 86, 114, 123

Agility, 31, 32, 57, 81, 84, 98, 129; hockiness and, 83

Alden, Steve: photo by, 103, 104, 109

Alfalfa, 120, 121, 122, 123–24

Alfonse, story about, 53

Alpi, story about, 39

Alpine conditions, surviving in, 96–101, 131. *See also* Cold tolerance

Alpine ibex (*Capra ibex*), 135

Alpines, 26, 34, 133; breed characteristics of, 134–35; crossbreeding with, 36; Flehman Response by, 32; growth patterns of, 124; heat-tolerance of, 95, 134, 136; packing with, 30–33; photo of, 31, 32; varieties of, 135

American Alpines, 30; breed characteristics of, 134. *See also* Alpines

American Dairy Goat Association, 31, 36, 135

American Elder Hostel, 15

Angoras, 26, 27, 85; photo of, 27

Animal protein, craving for, 90

Anoxia, 92

Antibiotics, 44

Apocynin, 57

Appropriate technology, 5–6

Arnica liniment, 44

Back, Joe, 15

Back, Mary, 15

Backcountry: protecting, 52; trips in, 56–57, 97

Backpacking, 97; alternatives to, 4–5, 7, 9, 14–15, 16, 23; right of way and, 58

Bad habits: breaking, 114–15; learning, 108

Bag Balm, 44

Bars, description of, 41

Bedouins, Nubian goats and, 137

Behavior, 56, 57, 137; problems with, 30; studying, 55, 68–71

141

Behavior modification, 105, 107, 113–15. *See also* Rewards
Bells, using, 53, 55, 60, 64, 119
Bellwethers, 60
Benzaldehyde poisoning, symptoms of, 75
Bezoar (*Capra aegagrus*), 127; description of, 132–33. *See also* Wild goats
Bighorn sheep, 93, 96, 132; diet of, 78; diseases from, 100. *See also* Rocky Mountain bighorn sheep
Biting, discouraging, 73
Body temperature, maintaining, 91–92, 131–32
Bonding: feeding and, 103; importance of, 32, 35, 51, 55–57, 64, 103, 105, 107
Bottle-feeding, bonding and, 103
Breakaway, using, 66–67
Breast collar, 60; using, 41, 47
Breed characteristics, 26–36; developing, 134–38; wild origins of, 129
Breeders, 22, 29, 31, 34, 53, 90–91, 113, 137; C.A.E. and, 125; horn removal and, 85; improvements by, 36, 61; tips from, 76; training and, 105; working with, 56, 102, 124
Breeding goats, caring for, 122
British Harness Goat Society, 16
Browsing, 60, 63, 64, 118, 120
Bureau of Land Management, 18
Butting, 86–88; discouraging, 73; social order and, 86. *See also* Horns

C.A.E. (Caprine arthritis and encephalitis), prevention of, 125
Calcium: problems from, 78–79; reducing, 123
Camels: desert conditions and, 89; hooves of, 91
Capra, 1; members of, 81
Capra prisca, 128, 136–37
Caprid esters, 98

Caprine arthritis and encephalitis. *See* C.A.E.
Caproic acid, 69
Caseous lymphadenitis, description of, 125–26
Cashmeres, 26, 27, 28, 85, 131, 134; heat-tolerance of, 94
Casper, story about, 36
Castor bean plants, 75
Castration, late, 113
Chafing. *See* Saddle sores
Chamois, 30, 31, 33, 96, 128, 130; breed characteristics of, 135–36, 138; heat-tolerance of, 136
Chamoisee, 31, 135
Chokecherries, 75–76
Christmas trees, as supplemental feed, 122–23
Cigar therapy, using, 114
Cinches, 60; using, 41–42, 46–47, 48
COB (corn, oats, barley), 59, 99, 105, 108, 120, 123
Coefficient of sliding friction, 81, 82. *See also* Traction
Cold-tolerance, 61–62, 63, 129, 131, 135. *See also* Alpine conditions; Heat-tolerance
Color patterns, 31, 33, 135
Commercial outfitters. *See* Outfitters
Companionship, 14, 16, 19–22, 32, 38, 50–52, 105, 112, 117, 118, 138
Conditioning, importance of, 56, 63, 66, 79, 112, 138. *See also* Exercising
Conway buckle, 47
Corney, Jeff: photo by, 59, 93, 101
Cou Blanc, 31
Cou Claire, 31
Crossbreeding, 30, 35, 94–95, 135, 135n, 138; success with, 36
Crossbucks, 43, 47, 48; description of, 41–42
Cud, chewing, 130
Curiosity, development of, 132
Cyanide poisoning, symptoms of, 75

Dairy goats, 2, 23, 29, 31, 35–36, 80, 85, 94, 102, 122

Dealers. *See* Breeders

Decker. *See* Pack pad

Defense, methods of, 68–69, 86–88

Dehydration, 100; preventing, 91

Desert conditions, adapting to, 89–95, 131, 136

Desertification, 2, 60

Dewclaws, traction and, 82–84

Diet, 63, 75–76, 130; maintaining, 61, 121–23, 138; observing, 78. *See also* Food

Digestion, 90, 130; adaptation in, 132

Diseases, 100; working against, 124–26

Distemper, immunity to, 53

Dogs, 127; encounters with, 23, 51, 57, 105, 119, 121

Domestic goats: adaptability of, 132–33; origins of, 8, 74–75, 89, 127–28

Dominance. *See* Pecking order

Dominant female, role of, 69–70

Dominant male, 73; role of, 69–70

Donkeys, 7, 19

Douglas, Steve: photo by, 77

Drinking, 94

Drought tolerance, 89–90, 131, 138

Eating. *See* Feeding

Education, 14–15

Endurance, 30, 94, 138

Environmental damage: goats and, 23–25; limiting, 52, 60, 74

Equipment, description of, 40–44

Erosion, 3, 52

Etiquette, rules of, 58

Excess energy, working off, 115

Exercising, 112; need for, 79, 82. *See also* Conditioning

Exposure, 100, 129

Eyesight, keenness of, 16, 18, 30, 87, 92, 129, 130

Feeding, 20, 23–25, 63, 75–76; adaptation in, 132; bonding and, 103; instinct for, 76; opportunistic, 97–98; regulating, 115; supplementary, 99–100, 120, 121–24

Fences, building, 118–20

Flehman Response: description of, 32; photo of, 32

Food, preferences for, 74–76, 78–80, 90. *See also* Diet

French Alpines, 30, 33; breed characteristics of, 134, 135; heat-tolerance of, 136. *See also* Alpines

Gentian violet, 44

Genticin ointment, 44

Glaciers, goats and, 97–100, 131

Goat-antelopes, 30, 33, 96, 128, 129, 130, 135n; pack strings and, 68; predators and, 69

Goat-keeping, 13, 18, 20, 53, 58–59, 61–63, 117–26

Goat-packing: breeds for, 26; discovering, 4–5, 8–9, 18, 19–25; early, 38–39; education about, 14–15; reactions to, 39–40

Goat, definition of, 1

Grain, providing, 63, 115. *See also* Feeding

Grain bell, using, 64

Graupel: preference for, 98; recipe with, 101

Grazing potential, improving, 118, 119

Group order. *See* Pecking order

Growth, stunting, 124

Guardian. *See* Watch goats

Habitat requirements, 118–19

Hardware poisoning, preventing, 126

Hay, 120, 122, 123, 124

Head halter, 100

Health, maintaining, 80, 102, 124–26, 138

Heart rate, increased, 57–58

Heat-tolerance, 30, 85, 93–95, 129, 134–38. *See also* Cold-tolerance; Overheating

Hegg, E. A.: photo by, 27
Herd instinct, maintaining, 112
Hitches, description of, 48–50
Hockiness: description of, 33–34; stability and, 83
Hooves: caring for, 56, 79, 81–84, 121; resilience of, 85; toughening, 82
Horns: breed determination and, 85–88; defense with, 86–88; grabbing, 108; physiological role of, 88, 88n, 92, 132; removing, 85, 86, 120. *See also* Butting
Horse-packers: hitches of, 48; problems for, 6–7; reactions of, 39; right of way for, 58
Horses, 97; desert conditions and, 89; digestion by, 90; eating habits of, 23–24; encounters with, 53, 105; packing with, 5–6, 9, 12, 38; problems with, 7, 15, 19, 46; upkeep for, 6–7; wild, 93
Horses, Hitches, and Rocky Trails (Back), 15
Housing, building, 120–21
Huckleberries, 101
Hypothermia, recognizing, 61–62

Independent streaks, dealing with, 112
Instincts, understanding, 70–71, 76, 112
Intelligence, 22, 61, 137

Jacobsen's organ, 32
Jessie, story about, 11
Johnson, Frandee: photo by, 22, 24, 79, 113
Julio, snuggling with, 14
Jumping, 109–10, 111
Jupiter, story about, 14, 15

Keyhole mangers, building, 121–22
Kidding ground, 69, 70
Kids, 2, 11, 119; milk for, 123; protecting, 69, 70; training, 68, 102, 105, 107, 108, 138

Kinder, 26, 28
Knife, carrying, 44
Knoodling, 21–22, 112. *See also* Petting

LaManchas, 26; breed characteristics of, 137–38; crossbreeding with, 36; heat-tolerance of, 95, 134, 137–38; packing with, 34–35
Laurels, 75–76
Lazy goats, 56, 137
Lead goats, 67–70, 72; teaching, 107, 111
Lead rope, 44, 50, 66, 100, 111; shortening, 73, 107; using, 45, 51, 55
Llama-packers: hypothermia and, 62; right of way for, 58
Llamas, 12, 13, 97, 100, 109; costs of, 19; encounters with, 105; packing with, 7–8; problems with, 19–20
Load, 40–50, 56, 65; balancing, 45–46; removing, 59–60; securing, 48
Lungworm, 100

Mangers, building, 121–22
Mantying, 43, 49–50
Markhor (*Capra falconeri*), 127
Medicinal plants, 78
Migrations, 69–70, 71, 73
Milk: benefits of, 11; pasteurizing, 125; poison in, 76; using, 9, 13, 20, 101, 101n
Milk goats, 11, 117, 136; horn removal for, 85, 86
Milk production, 11, 35–36, 79, 98; breeding for, 134
Mineral block, carrying, 100. *See also* Salt
Mischief, encountering, 115–16
Mohair, 131
Mountain goats, 78, 96, 130; diseases from, 100
Mules, 19, 22
Musculature, developing, 10–11. *See also* Conditioning; Exercising

National Outdoor Leadership School (NOLS), 14
National Park Service, 18
Neck collars, 100; description of, 43–44
Night vision. *See* Eyesight
NOLS. *See* National Outdoor Leadership School
Nubian ibex (*Capra ibex nubiana*), 131
Nubians, 26, 34; breed characteristics of, 136–37; heat-tolerance of, 93, 94, 136; packing with, 35–36, 137; photo of, 35; problems with, 55–56, 137; training, 55–56
Nutrition. *See* Diet

Oberhaslis, 26; crossbreeding with, 36; growth patterns of, 124; heat-tolerance of, 95, 136; packing with, 33–34, 135; photo of, 33; varieties of, 135; water and, 55
Off-trail conditions, training for, 57–58
Ornamental oleander, 75
Osteoporosis, 79
Oster, Jerri: photo by, v
Cutfitters, goat-keeping by, 18–19, 124–25
Overfeeding, 79
Overgrazing, 2, 3, 8, 20, 74
Overheating, 56; horns and, 88, 88n, 92; preventing, 91. *See also* Heat-tolerance
Overloading, 56

Pack animals, 1; acquiring, 6–8, 22–23; laws regarding, 52; prices of, 7, 22–23
Pack bags, description of, 43
Pack covers, 60; description of, 43
Pack goats, 2; description of, 9–10; efficiency of, 23–25; healthiness of, 80; sources of, 36
Packing techniques, 39; description of, 40–50

Pack pad, description of, 41
Pack string, arrangement of, 66, 67, 70–73
Pack train. *See* Pack string
Panniers, 43, 47–48, 50, 57; balancing, 45–46, 64; removing, 59; securing, 49; training with, 112
Pecking order, sorting out, 32, 67, 68, 70–73, 86, 92, 116
Pelletized alfalfa/grain mix, using, 59, 99–100. *See also* Feeding, supplementary
Personality, 34, 35, 36, 57, 112, 137
Peters, John and Laura: photo by, 33
Petting, 14, 21–22, 59, 62, 103, 105, 107, 112. *See also* Knoodling
Picket breaking, 60, 61, 107
Plants: medicinal, 78; poisonous, 57–58, 74, 75–76, 130; selecting, 76, 78
Playing, 84, 100, 103, 105
Poisonous plants, 57–58; checking for, 76; death from, 75–76; tolerance for, 74, 130
Predators, 51, 57, 98, 129; defense against, 68–70, 86–87, 118, 121; vulnerability to, 131
Pronghorns, 68, 93, 132; diseases from, 100
Protector patterns, development of, 113–15
Pumpkin seeds, salt from, 95
Punishment, 105, 113–16. *See also* Training
Pygmy, 26, 27, 85, 102
Pygora, 26, 27, 28

Racial clines, 131, 135
Range, expanding, 129–31
Range improvement, goats and, 118, 119
Range of thermoneutrality, extending, 91–92, 131–32
Renting, 12, 14, 23, 53, 117
Reproduction, rate of, 2, 103
Resting, 58–60, 62–63, 92, 98–99

Rewards, giving, 59–60, 64, 95, 105, 107, 123. *See also* Behavior modification
Right of way, determining, 58
Rocky Mountain bighorn sheep, 98; diet of, 76; horn-butting by, 88; observing, 8–11. *See also* Bighorn sheep
Roles, accepting, 70–73
Rump strap, 41, 47
Rupicapra, 129, 135

Saanens, 26, 30, 31, 46, 133, 135; alpine conditions and, 100; breed characteristics of, 134; crossbreeding with, 29, 36; growth patterns of, 124; heat-tolerance of, 93–94, 134; packing with, 28–29, 134; photo of, 28; problems with, 28–29; sun-basking by, 93
Saddlebucks, 49, 66
Saddle pad: description of, 42–43; using, 46
Saddles: description of, 41–42; homemade, 41; training with, 112; using, 46–47, 59, 65
Saddle sores, 56; sources of, 46, 47
Safety, practicing, 73
Salt, carrying, 95
Sawbuck, description of, 41
Scapegoats, 3
Schilling, Gail: photo by, 118
Sheds, building, 120–21
Sheep, goats and, 98, 118
Siberian ibex (*Capra ibex sibirica*), 128, 134
Sled goats, 93
Snow, preference for, 98
Social order. *See* Pecking order
Sores. *See* Saddle sores
Spanish ibex (*Capra pyrenaica*), 127, 137
Spooking, 13, 46
Stones, 80; developing, 78–79
Straps, 41–42
String. *See* Pack string

Stringing, proper, 66, 67–68
Sun-basking, 93
Sungau, 31
Supplementary feeding. *See* Feeding, supplementary
Surprise, using, 113–15, 116
Sweating, 92, 94, 132
Swimming. *See* Water, fear of
Swiss Alpines. *See* Alpines
Swiss chamois (*Rupicapra rupicapra*). *See* Chamois
Switchbacks, cutting, 52

Talking, 46, 55, 59, 105, 107, 112. *See also* Verbal commands
Tarps, using, 49–50
Tethering, 60–61, 64
Thermoneutrality. *See* Range of thermoneutrality
Thiocyanate transulferase, 75
Tibet, goat-packing in, 38
Tin Cup, story about, 113–14
Toe holds, 83
Toggenburgs, 10, 26, 30, 31, 133, 135; alpine conditions and, 100; breed characteristics of, 134; crossbreeding with, 36; Flehman Response by, 32; growth patterns of, 124; heat-tolerance of, 94, 134; independent streak in, 112; packing with, 29–30; photo of, 29; training, 30
Toggen Daz Glacier Ice Cream, making, 101
Top load, 43, 47–48
Toxic plants. *See* Poisonous plants
Traction, 81–82; dewclaws and, 83
Trail rules, 52, 58
Training, 13, 16, 19, 22, 30, 35, 36, 59–60, 67, 71, 73, 84, 98, 102–3, 107–16, 123, 138; breeders and, 55, 105; conditioning and, 112; early, 108; importance of, 55–56; limits on, 107; pack, 110–12; responding to, 57, 113. *See also* Punishment; Verbal commands

Tree, description of, 41
Tundra, goats and, 97–98
Twain, Mark, 5

U.S. Forest Service, 8, 18; pack-
animal laws by, 52, 109
Urea, recycling, 25, 90, 92
Urine-spraying, 69

Vaccinations, 124
Verbal commands, 57, 73. *See also*
Talking; Training
Versatility, 7–8, 19, 31, 32, 57, 81,
129
Veterinarians, checkup with, 100,
124–25
Veterinary kit, 120; contents of, 44
Vomero-nasal organ, 32

Walia ibex (*Capra walie*), 96, 131
Watch goats, 30, 36, 70, 73, 137
Water, 46, 100; conserving, 90,
91–92, 94, 98; fear of, 55, 73,
107–11

Waterproofing, 49–50
Weaning, 123
Weed control, 76, 118, 119
Wethers: calcium and, 123; eating
habits of, 23–25; growth patterns
of, 124; independent streak in,
112; keeping, 9, 112, 117–18, 122;
training, 113–14
Wethervane, packing with, 9–11
Wild cherries, 75–76
Wilderness trips, goat-packing on, 12,
56–57, 97
Wild goats, 30, 94, 127–29, 134;
adaptations by, 131; dewclaws
and, 82; habitat of, 80; hockiness
of, 33–34; pack strings and, 67–68;
societies of, 68–71; survival rate
of, 84. *See also* Bezoar
Working fatigue, 56, 134; value of,
111
Worming, 100, 126

Yogurt, 13; making, 11